THE PLAY OF GEORGE ORWELL'S

ANIMAL FARM

Adapted by Peter Hall

with lyrics by Adrian Mitchell
music by Richard Peaslee

Notes and questions by
Andrew Worrall

HEINEMANN
EDUCATIONAL

PREFACE

In this edition of Peter Hall's dramatisation of *Animal Farm* you will find notes, questions and activities to help in studying the play, particularly as part of a GCSE course.

The introduction provides background information on George Orwell and on the historical and political basis of his fable. It discusses the relationship between the fable and this play.

The activities at the end of the book range from straightforward *Keeping Track* questions which can be tackled at the end of each act, or during it, to focus close attention on what is happening in the play, through more detailed work on characters and themes in *Explorations,* to more advanced discussion questions under *Criticism.*

There is also a bibliography to assist in the further study of George Orwell's work.

CONTENTS

INTRODUCTION

When was the last time you read a book in which the characters were talking animals? Can you imagine appearing on the stage dressed as an animal? Horses, hens and pigs who act like people would seem to belong to nursery school books, Christmas pantomimes and cartoon films.

There is a tradition in adult literature, however, of using animals as a vehicle for commenting on human behaviour, often in a highly critical way. In mediaeval Europe animal fables such as *Reynard the Fox* were a way of satirising human greed, cunning and the misuse of power. One of Geoffrey Chaucer's pilgrims in *The Canterbury Tales*, The Nun's Priest, tells just such a story concerning farmyard poultry and a fox. At the beginning of the eighteenth century Jonathan Swift, the author of *Gulliver's Travels*, created a race of horses called the Houyhnhnms (pronounced whinnhims) to represent all that is virtuous and reasonable. He portrayed them as ruling a depraved and inferior breed, the Yahoos, who are uncomfortably reminiscent of humanity. All these stories are satires: they take recognisable aspects of human behaviour and, by exaggerating them, are able to comment upon them. The audience may be amused and simultaneously, perhaps, horrified. The aim of satire is to encourage us to change the way we think and behave.

Why should George Orwell have revived this tradition when he wrote *Animal Farm*? He subtitled the book 'A Fairy Story' and intended it to be read as a fable but if we are to understand it we must consider both Orwell's biography and the events in European history through which he had lived.

George Orwell

George Orwell did not become what his parents had hoped and expected. When he started to publish books he changed his name – he was christened Eric Arthur Blair – and this act seems to be a symbol of the way in which he deliberately rejected his background and upbringing.

His father, Richard Blair, was a middle-aged civil servant working for the Indian Government. Eric was born in Bengal in 1903 and his mother returned to England with him in the following year. Eric's father did not permanently rejoin the family until his retirement in 1911, by which time the boy had been sent away to board at preparatory school. Father and son never became close.

The Blair family might be described as genteel middle class and was sufficiently wealthy to send Eric to an expensive school, St Cyprian's, which would prepare him for Eton. Though he seems to have been quite popular and academically able he wrote later of his deep unhappiness at school. He suffered from a chest illness (which would affect him for the rest of his life) and he was bullied. At Eton he had some sporting success but did little work. In some respects he admired the school but his education left him with a profound consciousness of snobbery, hypocrisy and the pretensions of the British social class system. He learnt to sympathise with the underdog.

His academic achievements at Eton were insufficient to earn him the scholarship to university which his parents might have expected. Instead he joined the Imperial Indian Police and from 1922 to 1927 served as an officer in Burma. It was an experience which he came to dislike intensely. Imperialism seemed to be an extension of the autocratic school system, subjecting an entire population to the whims of a far-from-laudable foreign ruling class. He resigned and returned to Europe where, despite parental displeasure, he devoted himself to becoming a writer. He taught and did shop work to make ends meet but at first he lived largely in poverty, washing dishes in a Paris hotel and tramping across southern England. His account of these events, *Down and Out in Paris and London* (published in 1933 under the name George Orwell), demonstrates his total rejection of the attitudes and values of his middle-class upbringing and his identification with the very poor.

Orwell's personal odyssey reflects, in an exaggerated way, the challenge that was being faced by all thinking people at this time. Following the disaster of the First World War Europe had fallen into a major economic depression: one in eight people in the British labour force was out of work by 1931. Meanwhile, in Russia, the communist revolution of 1917 had seemed to offer the vision of a new world which would do away with the divisions of social class and economic slavery, being built upon a belief in human equality. Many of Orwell's contemporaries sympathised with socialism and joined the Labour or Communist parties.

Orwell joined the Independent Labour Party in 1938 though he was never a conventional socialist; rather he was responding to the rise of the two powerful totalitarian regimes which would direct the course of European history for the rest of his life, Hitler's Germany and Stalin's Russia.

Totalitarian governments, usually dominated by a single leader and an inner political elite, deprive individual citizens of their rights, permit no opposition and remain in power through the use of military force and propaganda. During the thirties Orwell published novels, essays and studies which showed his sympathy for the down-trodden and the hopeless but which did not advocate a consistent political programme. However in 1936 the Spanish Civil

War broke out and Orwell went to Barcelona to report on it and to fight. The experience gave a new focus to his work and he wrote later that 'Every line of serious work I have written since 1936 has been written, directly or indirectly, *against* totalitarianism and *for* democratic socialism, as I understand it.' (*Why I Write,* 1947)

What he experienced in Spain was a war between the Popular Front government, which included socialists, and the right-wing Nationalist forces of General Franco backed by the fascist governments of Italy and Germany. The Popular Front was supported by socialist volunteers (like Orwell) from many countries but received little help from Russia; indeed it seemed to be Stalin's policy to undermine the Front government. Orwell's account, *Homage to Catalonia,* vividly contrasts the comradeship of the ordinary soldiers with the treachery on the politicians of all sides.

Orwell was wounded and returned to England more than ever determined to fight in whatever way he could against political extremism, whether of the right or the left. He was not fit enough for military service in the Second World War but joined the Home Guard and produced talks for the BBC Empire department. At the end of 1943 he started writing *Animal Farm* and completed it within three months. The book was published in 1945 and became an immediate success. For the first time Orwell was earning sufficient money to be able to concentrate entirely on writing. His major work of the post-war years, *1984,* is a deeply pessimistic account of the imagined universal rise of totalitarianism. By the time *1984* was published Orwell was terminally ill with tuberculosis and he died on 23 January, 1950.

Animal Farm: A Fairy Story

Orwell's biography suggests that we should not expect *Animal Farm* to make us feel comfortable. One of its achievements is that it makes difficult situations and ideas accessible through the deceptive simplicity of the story. Orwell was very clear that this was his intention. In a preface to the Ukrainian edition of the book he wrote:

> On my return from Spain I thought of exposing the Soviet myth in a story that could be easily understood by almost anyone and which could be easily translated into other languages. However the actual details of the story did not come to me for some time until one day (I was then living in a small village) I saw a little boy, perhaps ten years old, driving a huge cart-horse along a narrow path, whipping it whenever it tried to turn. It struck me that if only such animals became aware of their strength we should have no power over them, and that men exploit animals in much the same way as the rich exploit the proletariat.

> (Quoted in Crick, B. *George Orwell: a life* (1980) p. 309)

If we are to understand 'the Soviet myth' we need to look briefly at Soviet history and relate it to the characters of *Animal Farm*.

Orwell's Manor Farm represents Russia. From the seventeenth to the early twentieth century Russia was ruled by the Romanov Tsars ('Mr Jones'). For most of that time the agricultural labourers (the farm animals), who were the majority of the population, were slaves, known as serfs; even after serfdom was abolished in 1861 the Tsar continued to hold absolute power. Most Russians lived under conditions of considerable hardship and the suffering of many during the early years of the First World War was the final spur to revolution.

The Russian Revolution of 1917 was the work of a group called the Bolsheviks, dominated by its leader, Lenin (1870–1924). His political ideas were based on the writings of Karl Marx (1818–83) and Friedrich Engels (1820–95). Their pamphlet, *The Communist Manifesto* (1848) described how and why it was inevitable that oppressed workers – the proletariat – would overthrow the ruling bourgeoisie and take for themselves in common all land and the means of industrial and agricultural production. The resulting classless society would benefit all members equally since each would work and receive benefit according to individual abilities and needs. Marx, Engels and Lenin are combined in the character of Old Major whose speech ('Last night I had a strange dream . . . ') is the animals' manifesto.

Under Communism (Animalism) personal wealth was to be outlawed and those who hankered after it would be considered enemies of the state (Mollie). Religion, which offered hope of heaven after death, was seen to distract people from the task of creating a perfect society here and now. The Russian church (Moses) was outlawed and its property seized.

Between 1917 and 1921 counter-revolutionary forces – the White Russians – tried to provide effective military resistance. They were helped by several countries, including Britain, France and Japan (represented by Mr Pilkington in the play), but defeated by the Red Army which was largely the creation of Lenin's deputy, Trotsky (Snowball). Once the Revolution had succeeded the Cheka (the Dogs) was established to silence dissident voices. Renamed the OGPU and later the NKVD and KGB it became a secret police force responsible for the imprisonment and death of millions of Russians.

Following Lenin's death in 1924 a period of internal rivalry within the inner circles of the Communist party ended with Stalin (Napoleon) seizing the reins of power and forcing Trotsky into exile in 1929. Stalin eventually had

Trotsky murdered. Lenin's body was kept on public view in Moscow, much as Old Major's skull was cleaned and nailed to a pole.

Post-revolutionary Russia was industrially and economically backward. From 1928 onwards 'Five-Year Plans' were designed to develop the nation's resources (The Windmill) and it was politically essential that each plan was seen by the Russian people and the outside world to have succeeded, even when it had not. Stalin came to rely increasingly on a sophisticated control of information to convey the message that Communism was achieving its aims. His propagandists (Squealer) used the press, literature, film and even architecture, painting and music to bolster confidence in the state and its infallibility. Original thought was suppressed, replaced by slogans ('Four legs good, two legs better').

By the nineteen-thirties it was becoming clear that Stalin and the inner circle of the Communist party (the pigs) had betrayed the ideals of Marxist-Leninism and would do anything to suppress opposition and maintain the security of the USSR. Stalin held 'show trials' in order to remove people who did not agree with him (the trials of the hens and other animals).

For Orwell and many of a similar mind the dream of communism was over and they could only watch in despair as the world divided itself into opposing power blocks. It must have seemed to him, as he started to write *Animal Farm* in the depths of war, that none of his hopes for humanity would be realised: the poor would remain exploited, pawns in conflicts they could not control; new empires would arise from the ashes of the old; democracy would give way to the requirements of fulfilling war aims; the people would be governed by secrecy and propaganda and even if fascism were defeated a new war would break out between the capitalist allies and Stalinist Russia. It would not matter in which country one lived: the animals would remain oppressed while pig and man became indistinguishable.

The fairy story thus became a nightmare. Stalin did not die until 1953 so Orwell never saw reason to revise his opinion. Even if he had lived to see the discrediting of Stalin he would have found no cause for hope in the behaviour of Khrushchev and Brezhnev, his successors, who brutally suppressed democratic reforms in Hungary in 1956 and Czechoslovakia in 1968. *Animal Farm* is an allegory of European history through much of the twentieth century.

We have witnessed the collapse of the Soviet Empire in recent years but that is not a reason for disregarding the book's message since Orwell also intended that it could be understood in other ways.

At the simplest level it is a fable about the way in which people may seize and keep power. Jones neglects the animals, leaving them in a state to respond to leadership, however untrustworthy that leadership may be. Once in power Napoleon uses a combination of military strength and propaganda to suppress opposition. This is, suggests Orwell, the story of all revolutions and he clearly had in mind the French Revolution which was subverted by Napoleon Bonaparte. You may like to consider how far the comparison holds good if you examine events since Orwell's death such as the history of Communist China or recent developments in Eastern Europe.

The nature and power of propaganda is also a major theme for Orwell. During the Second World War he had direct experience of the way in which the British propaganda machine worked to make people believe in the aims of the war and to keep up morale. He was also well aware of how the German Minister of Enlightenment, Joseph Goebbels, used propaganda to maintain support for the Nazi party. This was based on Hitler's dictum that the mass of the people 'will more easily fall victims to a great lie than to a small one' (*Mein Kampf*). Squealer's lies are never small: he 'could turn black into white'. Propaganda is not only used by totalitarian states. Even in a liberal democracy the mass media bombards us with statements claiming to be 'truths'.

A crucial purpose of education is to make us more able to discriminate truth from falsehood. What makes the majority of the animals so gullible is their ignorance, apathy and self-delusion. Even those who are literate fail to use the power at their disposal because they lack their own vision and the resolve to pursue it. This is not merely a criticism of political blindness: it is a very pessimistic analysis of human nature in general and suggests that Orwell had little expectation that we would be able to heed his warning.

Animal Farm: the play

In their dramatisation Peter Hall and Adrian Mitchell add a further level of reference, the importance of which Orwell would not have foreseen in 1943 but which I believe he would have approved. He had a strong love for the British landscape and in Mitchell's song 'The Green Flag' and Hall's reworking of the final scene we are asked to see the animals not just as surrogate human beings but as animals in their own right, asserting the integrity of the natural world and the harm that man's ill-considered intervention can do to it.

In other respects you will find this adaptation very faithful to the book. One or two minor characters have been omitted, some scenes compressed and details changed for dramatic reasons but Hall follows the order of the plot so that it is easy and instructive to make a comparison between the original novel and the play. Orwell's original narrative includes some long speeches but relatively little dialogue. Look at the techniques which Hall uses to make it into a convincing and fast moving piece of drama. Mitchell's lyrics take greater liberties with Orwell's prose, but he retains some songs such as 'Beasts of England' and 'Comrade Napoleon' which Orwell wrote.

A play with music has a special kind of impact. The songs allow reflection upon the situation as well as changing the emotional temperature. They contrast with and complement the rapidly moving sequence of events.

A good production of *Animal Farm* will catch our attention, amuse and horrify, and encourage us to suspend our disbelief of talking animals and walking pigs. If we then choose to reflect upon what we have experienced it may also be that *Animal Farm* will make us more aware, and wary, of the political and social forces to which we are subject.

Andrew Worrall

List of Characters

THE BOY

MR JONES

OLD MAJOR: a large old pig

BOXER: a huge cart horse

CLOVER: a stout motherly mare

MURIEL: a white goat

BENJAMIN: an old donkey

MOLLIE: a foolish, pretty white mare

SNOWBALL: a young, vivacious boar

NAPOLEON: a young boar of deep character

SQUEALER: a small fat porker

THE CAT

MOSES: a tame raven

MINIMUS: a pig with a gift for composing songs
                    and poems

THREE YOUNG PIGS

FOUR SHEEP

THREE COWS

TWO HENS

A BULL

TWO PIGEONS

MR WHYMPER

MR PILKINGTON

DOGS, FARMERS, OTHER MEN AND ANIMALS

Cast of the 1984 National Theatre Production

Animal Farm was first performed at the Cottesloe Theatre, London, on 25 April 1984 by the National Theatre with the following cast:

BOXER/FARMER	Geoffrey Burridge
CAT/NAPOLEON'S DOG/HEN/PIGEONS	Kate Dyson
HEN/COW/MRS JONES/PIG	Jenny Galloway
THE BOY	Kamlesh Gupta/ Christopher Howard
SNOWBALL/MR WHYMPHER	Greg Hicks
MR JONES/GOOSE	Paul Imbusch
OLD MAJOR/MR PILKINGTON/SHEEP	Kenny Ireland
SHEEP/FARMER	Bill Moody
MINIMUS/HEN	Wendy Morgan
MURIEL	Judith Paris
NAPOLEON	Barrie Rutter
SQUEALER	David Ryall
CLOVER	Dinah Stabb
MOSES/HEN/PIGEONS/FARMER	Paul Stewart
COW/PIG/STABLE LAD	Paul Tomany
MOLLIE/NAPOLEON'S DOG/HEN	Jessica Turner
BENJAMIN	Bev Willis

Directed by Peter Hall
Decor and masks by Jennifer Carey
Lighting by John Bury
Movement by Stuart Hopps
Musical direction by Matthew Scott
Sound by Caz Appleton

Animal Farm was subsequently performed in repertoire at the Olivier Theatre from 27 September 1984 to 3 April 1985 with an altered cast. It went to the Lyttleton Theatre on 2 September 1985 before touring Cardiff, Nottingham, Norwich, Bath, Plymouth, Manchester, Wolverhampton, Belfast and Hull.

A Note by the Adaptor

With judicious doubling, the play can be presented by a dozen actors. If more actors are available, they can be used to fill out the chorus of animals.

The original stage was completely black. Brightly coloured elements of the Farm – like pieces in a child's toy set – were moved about by black figures. The actors wore black, except for brightly coloured elements – their animal masks, tails and feet. Until the end of the play, they went on all fours, using crutches of varying heights on their hands. The 'human' characters also wore masks. This was one solution to the production of the play. There are many others.

Peter Hall
January 1985

ACT ONE

A BOY'S *bedroom. A large bookcase. A toy chest on it, a child's brightly coloured farm set.*

A BOY *some eight or nine years old strolls forward. He stands on a chair and selects a book from the top of the bookcase. He moves down stage and sits on the toy box.*

BOY (*reading*): *Animal Farm.* A fairy story by George Orwell.

The BOY'S *room disappears. The farmhouse and the farm gate take over the stage.* MR JONES *is revealed standing by the gate. On the gate is painted a slogan: 'Manor Farm'.*

'In the past Mr Jones, although a cruel master, had been a capable farmer. But now he spent more and more time in the Red Lion. Every night he came home drunk.

MR JONES (*singing*): **Who made the cows and sheep so meek?
Who feeds the cats and dogs their meat?
Who's the loving father
Of fur and feather?
Man, bounteous man! Wonderful man!**

BOY His farm was now thoroughly neglected. The fields were full of weeds and the animals were underfed and in poor condition.

MR JONES **Who guards his servants with a gun
And, when their time to leave has come,
Who leads pigs and horses
To slaughter houses?
Man, masterful man. Powerful man.**

BOY He went up the stairs, undressed and climbed unsteadily into bed.

Throughout the play what the BOY *describes happens around him. The black figures set elements of the farm, become animals, execute mimes, or speak scenes of dialogue.*

JONES *makes his way to the door of his house, kicks off his boots, and, still singing, goes up the stairs.*

Finally, the bedroom light goes out.

BOY As soon as the light was out, there was a stirring and a fluttering throughout the farm. Word had gone round the animals that there was to be a secret meeting in the big barn. Old Major, the stud boar had something to say . . .

Lights up on the barn full of animals. OLD MAJOR, *a large old pig, centre stage.* HENS, PIGEONS, SHEEP, COWS; BOXER, *a huge cart horse;* CLOVER, *a stout motherly mare;* MURIEL, *the white goat;* BENJAMIN, *the old donkey.*

MAJOR Last night I had a strange dream. Many years ago when I was a little pig, my mother and the other sows used to sing a secret and ancient song. I learnt that song. I learnt its words, I learnt its music. But it has long since passed out of my mind. Last night it came back to me. In my dream . . .

(*He sings*): **Beasts of England! Beasts of Ireland! Beasts of land and sea and skies! Hear the hoofbeats of tomorrow! See the golden future rise!**

The animals stir, but he quietens them.

Wait – no noise – wait! Or we'll wake up Jones! I am over twelve years old and have had over four hundred children. I think I understand the nature of life on this earth as well as any animal now living. Listen carefully, for I do not think that I shall be with you for many months longer.

MOLLIE, *a foolish pretty white mare, rushes in late.*

CLOVER Why are you late, Mollie?

MOLLIE Sorry . . . I had a stone in my hoof. (*She shrugs girlishly.*)

MAJOR Listen!

(*He sings*): **How does the life of an animal pass? In endless drudgery. What's the first lesson an animal learns? To endure its slavery.**

How does the life of an animal end?
In cruel butchery.

Is this simply part of the order of nature? No, comrades. This farm would support a dozen horses, twenty cows, hundreds of sheep – all of them living in comfort and dignity beyond our imagining. Our labour tills the soil, our dung fertilises it. And yet there is not one of us who owns more than his bare skin. The produce of our labour is stolen from us by human beings. Man is our only enemy.

He's the lord of all the animals
Yet he can't lay eggs or pull a plough.
He's the greatest of all criminals,
Stealing wool from the sheep and milk from the
**   cow.**
He's the lord of all the animals
And the only one who's no use.
For he consumes, consumes, consumes,
But he cannot produce.

Never listen when they tell you that man and the animals have a common interest – that the prosperity of the one is the prosperity of the other. You cows: what has happened to the milk which should feed you calves?

COWS   It has gone down the throat of our enemy! Man!

MAJOR   And you hens: what has happened to the eggs you have laid?

HENS   They have been stolen from us by our enemy! Man!

MAJOR   And you, Clover: where are your six children, the foals who should have been the support and pleasure of your old age?

CLOVER   They were sold at a year old by our enemy, man! I will never see them again.

MAJOR   But even the miserable lives that we lead are not allowed to reach their natural span. You young pigs will scream your lives out on the block within a year – every one of you.

Y'NG PIGS   (*in terror*): No! No! No!

MAJOR   Yes! To that horror we must all come. Cows, pigs, hens, sheep, everyone – even you Boxer. They'll butcher you.

BOXER   Why me? I work hard for them.

MAJOR   The day that those great muscles of yours lose their power, Jones will sell you to the knacker, who will cut your throat and boil you down for dog food. What must we do? Why, work, comrades. Work night and day, body and soul, for the overthrow of the human race! Rebellion! That is my message to you, comrades! Rebellion! I do not know when the rebellion will come, but I know as surely as I see the straw beneath my feet that sooner or later justice will be done. But when you conquer man do not adopt his vices. Remember that all animals are equal!

SNOWBALL   Old Major, what about the wild creatures – the rats and the rabbits – are they our friends or our enemies?

MAJOR   You must decide. You must learn to vote. Each one of you must have a say in the way we lead our lives. I propose this question to the meeting: Are the wild creatures comrades? All those in favour . . .

They begin to take a vote by raising their trotters and hooves. As the BOY *speaks the action freezes.*

BOY   And so the animals learnt to vote for the first time. It was agreed by an overwhelming majority that the wild creatures were comrades.

ALL   Agreed, agreed!

BOY   There was only one vote against: the cat. She was afterwards discovered to have voted on both sides.

MAJOR *and all* **THE ANIMALS: Beasts of England! Beasts of Ireland! Beasts of land and sea and skies! Hear the hoofbeats of tomorrow! See the golden future rise!**

Now the day of beasts is coming,
Tyrant man shall lose his throne
And the shining fields of England
Shall be trod by beasts alone.

Pull the rings from out of your noses!
Tear the saddle from your back!
Bit and spur shall rust forever,
Cruel whips no more shall crack.

Beasts of England, seize the prizes,
Wheat and barley, oats and hay,
Clover, beans and mangel wurzels
Shall be ours upon that day,
Shall be ours upon that –

MR JONES *flings open his bedroom window.*

MR JONES (*shouting*): QU-I-ET!

The ANIMALS *freeze, holding their breath.*

What's bothering you? Is it a fox? A fox, is it?

He reaches for his shotgun and fires into the darkness.

The lights fade as the meeting of the ANIMALS *breaks up quickly and silently.*

BOY Three nights later, Old Major died peacefully in his sleep.

The ANIMALS *watch as* OLD MAJOR *slowly leaves.*

His body was buried at the foot of the orchard.

Lights up. MR JONES *moves among the* ANIMALS, *cracking his whip.*

During the next three months, Jones continued to starve and bully them. But now the animals had a secret. They did not know when to expect the rebellion, but they believed fervently that one day it would come. The pigs, being the cleverest of the animals, led the preparation by organising and teaching.

NAPOLEON, SNOWBALL *and* SQUEALER *are seen teaching the* ANIMALS.

These three – Snowball, Squealer and Napoleon –
had elaborated Old Major's teachings into a
complete system of thought to which they gave the
name . . .

NAPOLEON, SNOWBALL *and* SQUEALER (*singing*):

> **Animalism . . ! Animalism . . ! Animalism . . !**

ALL   **Animalism!**

BOY   Snowball was an idealist, a pig who always dreamt
of perfecting the future . . .

SNOWBALL   A spectre is haunting England: the spectre of
Animalism. Animalism will lead us to the life of
plenty. Everything that we produce, we shall own –
collectively.

BOY   Squealer loved to talk . . .

SQUEALER   Information, comrades; facts, comrades; these are the
foundations of Animalism. Without knowledge, we
can have no opinions. And unless we have opinions,
we cannot vote. The majority must rule.

BOY   And Napoleon was a pig they all trusted . . .

NAPOLEON   I'm a practical pig, a pig of few words. So I'll work
hard and say little.

BOY   After Mr Jones was asleep, they all held secret
meetings in the barn.

SNOWBALL, SQUEALER *and* NAPOLEON *are holding their
meeting. They sing.*

SNOWBALL   **No man**
No master

SQUEALER   **Animals help each other**.

NAPOLEON   **Work fast**
Work faster

SNOWBALL   **Work for the future, brother.**

1ST COW   But Mr Jones feeds us.

2ND COW   If he were gone we should starve to death.

3RD COW   So we have to be loyal.

SNOWBALL **No! Animalism alters history!**
          Two-legged creatures are the enemy!
          Cows, sheep, chickens, cockerel, goose –
          Animals shall eat what animals produce!

NAPOLEON **No man**
          No killing
          What is our battle's sequel?

SNOWBALL (*sings*): **A land worth tilling.**
          All animals are equal.

CAT   I don't care what happens after I am dead.

SHEEP   If this rebellion is going to happen anyway, why
          should we work for it?

SQUEALER Try to understand, comrades. Allow yourselves to
          live by the spirit of Animalism.

SNOWBALL, SQUEALER *and* NAPOLEON: **No man**
          No master
          All animals are equal.

ALL   **No man**
          No master
          All animals are equal.

MOLLIE   Will there still be sugar after the rebellion?

SNOWBALL You don't need sugar. You will have all the oats and
          hay you want.

MOLLIE   But shall I still be able to wear ribbons in my
          mane?

SQUEALER Comrade, those ribbons are the badge of slavery.

SQUEALER Don't you understand that liberty is worth more than
          ribbons?

MOLLIE   (*unconvinced*): Yes, I suppose so. Couldn't I have
          some liberty ribbons?

BOY   The pigs had an even harder struggle to counteract
          the religious stories put about by Moses, Mr Jones'
          tame raven.

          MOSES *appears on a rafter. The* ANIMALS *quickly form
          into a respectful congregation.*

MOSES (*liturgically*): Believe me brethren. It's there, up in the sky!

> **Beyond the fences of this life**
> **There lies a wondrous hill**
> **And all good creatures when they die**
> **Go there to graze their fill.**

ALL **On Sugarcandy Mountain**
No labouring is done.
Beside a milky fountain
The beasts lie in the sun.
On Sugarcandy Mountain
You'll find the Treacle Lake
Lump sugar beyond counting
And fields of linseed cake.

> **So fear no more the knacker's yard**
> **Nor dread the abattoir**
> **But work today so you may join**
> **That Sugarcandy Choir.**

> **On Sugarcandy Mountain**
> **You'll find the Treacle Lake.**

SNOWBALL, SQUEALER *and* NAPOLEON (*as they break up the meeting*):
There's no such place as Sugarcandy
Mountain, No sweet by-and-by.
There's no such place as Sugarcandy Mountain,
Sugarcandy Mountain is a lie, lie, lie!
Sugarcandy Mountain is a lie!

SQUEALER **There's no such place as Sugarcandy Mountain,**
Animals are slaughtered and then
Converted into pork or mutton pies
Which are guzzled down the throats of men.

ALL **There's no such place as Sugarcandy Mountain,**
When you die you die.
There's no such place as Sugarcandy Mountain,
Sugarcandy Mountain is a lie. Lie, lie, lie!
Sugarcandy Mountain is a lie!
Is a mountainous, mountainous, mountainous
lie!

MOSES *leaves screaming in protest. The lights fade on the* ANIMALS.

BOY And so they went on waiting, waiting for the rebellion. Finally, it came sooner than anyone expected. One Saturday, Mr Jones got so drunk at the Red Lion that he did not come home till Sunday. And then he forgot to feed the animals . . .

MR JONES *returns drunk from the village. He ignores the pleas of the* ANIMALS, *and goes into the farmhouse.*

ALL Food! Where's our food? Give us food?

BOY Mr Jones immediately went to sleep on the drawing room sofa, with the *News of the World* over his face. When evening came, the animals were still unfed, and the barn doors were padlocked.

ALL (*in greater anguish*): Food! Where's our food? Give us food!

BOY At last they could stand it no longer.

Music. BOXER *kicks the barn door open, and the* ANIMALS *rush into it and begin to feed.* MR JONES *wakes up and comes into the yard. He confronts the* ANIMALS *with the whip. There is a moment of stillness. Suddenly, the* ANIMALS *fling themselves upon* MR JONES. *Their sudden uprising frightens him and he takes to his heels. He pushes open the farm gate and runs away down the road. The* ANIMALS *slam the gate behind him.*

And so, almost before they knew it had started, the rebellion was over. Manor Farm was theirs. They quickly wiped out all traces of the hated Jones.

MURIEL *tears the union jack from the flag pole and eats it.*

ALL Hooray!

BOXER *shakes off his straw hat and drops it over the gate.*

BOXER Just a gesture . . .

SNOWBALL *breaks the whip in two which* JONES *has discarded in the fight.*

ALL Hooray! Hooray! Hooray!

The ANIMALS *survey the farm.*

BOY They made a tour of inspection of the whole farm and surveyed with speechless admiration the ploughland, the hayfield, the orchard, the pool, the spinney. It was as though they had never seen these things before. And even now they could hardly believe that it was all their own. Then they filed back to the farm house and halted outside the door.

SNOWBALL *and* NAPOLEON *kick the door open and the* ANIMALS *cautiously enter the house.*

BOY They tiptoed from room to room afraid to speak above a whisper. They touched with awe the unbelievable luxury – the beds, the looking glasses, the sofa, the carpets, the lithograph of Queen Victoria. Mollie found a ribbon . . .

MOLLIE *takes a piece of blue ribbon from the dressing table, holds it against herself, and admires herself in the mirror.*

SQUEALER Ribbons are the mark of human beings. All animals should go naked . . .

BOY The pigs lifted down some hams hanging in the kitchen . . .

TWO YOUNG PIGS s*olemnly carry the hams out of the house in their teeth.*

NAPOLEON Let us give them decent burial.

The ANIMALS *hang their heads.*

SQUEALER I propose that this odious farmhouse should be preserved as a museum. The museum of man, the murderer. Let us put it to the vote.

ALL (*raising their trotters and hooves*): Agreed! Agreed!

SNOWBALL I have another proposal: is it agreed that no animals shall ever live here?

ALL Agreed! Agreed!

The lights fade. NAPOLEON *detaches himself from the rest of the* ANIMALS.

BOY   Mr Jones had four puppies, children of the guard dogs who had fled with him. Napoleon took the puppies away to a secret place, an old incubator shed behind the farmhouse. There, he fed them and looked after them. The rest of the farm soon forgot their existence.

Lights up. The ANIMALS *are all gathered round the five barred gate at the entrance to the farm.* SNOWBALL *holds a brush in his trotter. He has just finished painting a new name on the gate: 'Animal Farm'.*

BOY   And now Snowball revealed something wonderful . . .

SNOWBALL   Animal Farm!

BOXER   But how can you read? How can you write?

SQUEALER   During the time of preparation, we pigs taught ourselves to read and write . . .

SNOWBALL   From an old spelling book which belonged to Mr Jones' children . . .

NAPOLEON   We found it on the rubbish heap.

MOLLIE   (*reflectively*): It's a beautiful name, Animal Farm . . .

ALL   (*singing*): **'Animal Farm'.**

Lights out.

BOY   The pigs next explained that they had succeeded in reducing the principles of Animalism to seven commandments.

Lights up on the barn. SNOWBALL *is just painting slogan number seven on the lowest point of the wall.*

SNOWBALL	**ALL**
(*as he finishes painting*):	(*repeating*):
One.	**One.**
Two-legged beings are our enemies.	**Our enemies.**
Two.	**Two.**

Four-legged beings are allies and friends.	**Allies and friends.**
Three.	**Three.**
Animals shall never wear any clothes.	**Never wear clothes.**
Four.	**Four.**
Animals shall never sleep in beds.	**Never sleep in beds.**
Five.	**Five.**
Animals shall never drink alcohol.	**No alcohol.**
Six.	**Six.**
Animals shall never kill animals.	**Never kill animals.**
Seven.	**Seven.**
All animals are equal.	**All animals are equal.**

SNOWBALL These are the Seven Commandments. These are the unalterable Laws of Animal Farm.

ANIMALS Hooray!

SNOWBALL Comrades! Now that we are all equal, we are all equally responsible for the running of Animal Farm. So we must vote. And to vote, we must have opinions, be informed . . .

A SHEEP So do we have a leader?

SNOWBALL You are all leaders now. All leading Animal Farm to a bright and happy future.

ANOTHER SHEEP But who takes the decisions?

SNOWBALL We do.

CAT But what if I don't agree with the other leaders?

SNOWBALL But you will. The Majority is always right.

SHEEP Oh good!

NAPOLEON Don't worry, comrade. Just be practical. If we work hard, we shall not be hungry. And if we're not hungry, we shall worry less and argue less.

BOXER That's right, Napoleon. Comrade Napoleon is always right.

ANIMALS He is!

NAPOLEON Thank you, comrades.

SNOWBALL Now, comrades to the hayfield! Let's see if we can get the harvest in more quickly than Jones and his men.

There is a loud howl of protest from three COWS.

1ST COW Wait! We haven't been milked for twenty-four hours.

2ND COW My udder is about to burst.

3RD COW We can do nothing without men.

BOY So the pigs got buckets and milked the cows.

The PIGS *are seen milking the cows.*

They were very successful, because their trotters were well adapted to this task.

The PIGS *are seen carrying full buckets of milk.*

ANIMALS Hooray!

MOLLIE What will happen to all that milk?

NAPOLEON Never mind the milk, comrades. That will be attended to. The harvest is more important. Comrade Snowball will lead the way. I shall follow in a few minutes. Forward, comrades! The hay is waiting.

The ANIMALS *troop hesitantly off to the hayfield, as the lights fade. Only the* BOY *is left illuminated.*

BOY When they came back in the evening, the milk had disappeared. Every day it disappeared.

Lights up on SQUEALER *and the* ANIMALS.

SQUEALER Comrades! You do not imagine, I hope, that we pigs are taking the milk in a spirit of selfishness and privilege? Many of us actually dislike milk. I dislike it myself. Our sole object in mixing it in our mash is to preserve our health. Milk – this has been proved by science, comrades – contains substances absolutely necessary to the well-being of pigs. We pigs are brain workers. The whole management and organisation of this farm depends on us. Day and night we are watching over your welfare. It is for *your* sake that we drink the milk.

BOXER We never asked you to.

MURIEL And it was never voted on at a meeting.

ALL No!

MURIEL Does Snowball know about this?

SQUEALER Do you know what would happen if we pigs failed in our duty? Jones would come back! Yes, Jones would come back! Surely, comrades, surely there is no one who wants to see Jones back?

Consternation among the ANIMALS.

BOXER None of us wants to see Jones back.

SHEEP I propose the pigs be kept in good health.

ANIMALS (*voting*): Agreed! Agreed!

CLOVER It's in our own interest.

BOXER I propose that not only the milk, but the windfall apples when they come, and the main crop of apples when they ripen, should be reserved for the pigs.

ALL (*voting*): Agreed! Agreed!

SQUEALER Thank you, comrades.

Lights out.

BOY How they toiled and sweated to get the hay in!

Lights up.

SQUEALER Gee up, Boxer!

All the ANIMALS *freeze in horror.*

BOXER Comrade Squealer, don't say that. You sound like a man.

SQUEALER It may sound like that to you, comrade. But with our superior knowledge, it is natural that we pigs should direct the work and give the orders.

The ANIMALS *resume their work.*

BOY It was the biggest harvest the farm had ever seen. There was no wastage. The hens and ducks with their sharp eyes gathered up the very last stalk. And not an animal on the farm had stolen so much as a mouthful. There was plenty to eat.

Lights down, except for the BOY.

All through that summer, the animals were happy, happy as they had never thought possible.

Lights up. The ANIMALS *are feeding in a long line.*

SHEEP Now that the human beings have gone there is much more to eat.

CLOVER The food tastes better, because it's *our* food. We grew it ourselves.

MURIEL And it's not given to us by a mean and grudging master.

Lights down, except for the BOY.

BOY Boxer was the admiration of everybody. He had one answer to every problem, every setback . . .

Lights up. BOXER *strikes an heroic pose.*

BOXER I will work harder!

BOY This was now his personal motto. It was much admired.

Lights down, except for the BOY.

Everyone worked according to his capability. Nobody stole, nobody grumbled, or almost nobody.

Lights up.

SQUEALER Benjamin, aren't you happier without Jones?

BENJAMIN In Jones' time, I used to work hard every day. Now he's gone and everything's changed. And I still work hard every day.

BOY Nobody shirked. Or almost nobody.

SNOWBALL (*to* MOLLIE): Mollie, you were late again for work this morning.

SQUEALER And you left work early this afternoon.

MOLLIE There was another stone in my hoof.

ANIMALS (*snorting in contempt*): Huh!

Lights down, except for the BOY.

BOY   On Sundays there was no work. The day began at
            the flag pole.

Music. Lights up. MURIEL *hoists a flag on the flagstaff.*
It is a white hoof and horn on a green field.

ALL   **Our land was once a forest**
            All green from shore to shore
            Till humans tore the greenwood down
            With axe and fire and saw.

            But see! The banners of the grass are raised!
            The trees are striding through the dawn!
            And the green flag is flying
            With the signs of hoof and horn.
            Yes, man is fleeing from the countryside
            And soon our meadows shall be clean,
            For the green flag is flying
            And all England shall be green.
            Shall be green, shall be green, shall be green.

SNOWBALL The Hoof and Horn stand for the World Republic of
              the Animals which will be achieved when the
              human race has finally been overthrown.

ALL   Hooray!

SQUEALER The meeting is now open.

The ANIMALS *sit in a circle.*

SNOWBALL We will first take the reports from the Animal
              Committees. Every Committee, comrades, has
              exceeded expectation. Wherever I look, I see
              success. Particular praise is due to the hens, for their
              Egg Production Committee.

HENS   Thank you very much.

SNOWBALL To the sheep, for their White Wool Movement.

SHEEP   Thaaanks!

SNOWBALL And to the cows for their Clean Tails League.

COWS   Don't mention it.

NAPOLEON (*interrupting*): But I'm afraid we can't praise one

Committee. I have to report the failure of the Wild Comrades Re-education Committee.

BENJAMIN   The what?

SQUEALER   The Wild Comrades Re-education Committee.

SNOWBALL   It is the best of my ideas. Its purpose is to tame the rats and the rabbits and the birds, and all the wild creatures.

CAT   It has provided a wonderful opportunity. I have done much good work on the sparrows.

ALL   Well done! Well done!

A HEN   (*nervously*): I want to give a report on the Cat. She joined the Re-education Committee and was very active in it for some days. One day, I saw her sitting on the roof and talking to some sparrows. They were just out of her reach. She told them that as all animals are now equal, it was safe to come and perch on her paw. But the sparrows didn't believe her and kept their distance. Now the Cat no longer comes to the Re-education Committee. I want to know why, and I want to know now.

The HEN *and* CAT *confront each other, furious.*

NAPOLEON   (*rescuing the situation*): Comrades! Snowball is a brilliant pig. He inspires us all. But you can't expect that all his ideas will succeed. Now I'm a practical pig, a pig of few words. I believe that the future lies with the young. And I believe that the education of the young is more important than the re-education of anyone – wild or not. I have therefore made myself responsible for the education of the four puppies. Mr Jones' puppies. We must take care of the young.

ANIMALS   (*voting*): Agreed! Agreed!

BOXER   (*admiringly*): Napoleon is always right.

SNOWBALL   Napoleon *is* right. We must look after the young. But what about the old? I'm worried about the old animals. I propose that they be allowed to retire to a home of rest in the orchard.

ANIMALS (*voting*): Agreed! Agreed!

NAPOLEON But we can't do everything at once. We must be practical. We need every able-bodied animal to work.

SNOWBALL The old have earned some peace.

NAPOLEON Peace? This is wartime. We're surrounded by enemies. Everyone – old or young – must be trained in the use of fire-arms.

SNOWBALL No! That would be behaving like men. I will never agree to that. Remember Old Major. We must never behave like men. We must send out more and more pigeons to stir up rebellion on other farms.

A silence.

NAPOLEON If we cannot defend ourselves, we are bound to be conquered.

SNOWBALL If rebellions happen everywhere, we shall have no need to defend ourselves. I will not use a gun. You are wrong, Comrade Napoleon.

A silence.

How will you vote? All of you? I want your opinions. Who agrees with Napoleon? Who agrees with me? Boxer?

BOXER I am thinking it over.

SNOWBALL Benjamin? What do you think?

BENJAMIN Not me. I'm not going to start thinking at my age.

SNOWBALL Clover? Who do you think is right?

CLOVER I cannot make up my mind. I always find myself in agreement with the one who spoke last.

SNOWBALL But you must be responsible. You must start thinking for yourselves.

A silence.

NAPOLEON Let us be practical.

SQUEALER Yes! Let us go on with the meeting. Will you now all rise for the report on the Reading and Writing classes.

All the ANIMALS *rise.*

All the pigs can now read and write perfectly. No further work is necessary. I wish I could say the same for the rest of the animals. Muriel reads fairly well, but is only interested in reading from scraps of newspaper on the rubbish dump, which she consequently eats. It is suspected that Benjamin can read as well as the pigs.

BENJAMIN But as far as I know, there is nothing worth reading.

SQUEALER Clover has learnt the whole alphabet, but cannot put the words together. Boxer, however, is magnificent. Boxer, will you repeat the alphabet?

With difficulty, BOXER *traces out the capitals on the floor.*

BOXER Capital E . . . F . . . G . . . H . . .

He stops, staring at the letters.

SQUEALER You should be doing A, B, C, D, Boxer. You knew those last week.

BOXER *looks mortified.*

BOXER But this week, I have learnt capitals E, F, G, H . . .

SQUEALER Yes, but now you have learnt capitals E, F, G, H, you seem to have forgotten capitals A, B, C, D.

BOXER It's too difficult. I think I shall have to be content with the first four letters.

SQUEALER Capitals A, B, C, D?

BOXER (*repeating slowly and carefully*): Yes. Capitals A, B, C, D. It's the best I can do, yes, the best. I will write them out once or twice every day to keep them fresh in my memory. So I hope it will be an example.

SQUEALER And what about you, Mollie?

MOLLIE (*tracing the letters admiringly*): I know capitals M, and O. I know capital L and L; and capitals I and E.

SQUEALER Don't you know any more letters?

MOLLIE No. I only need to know the six letters which spell my name.

SQUEALER (*hiding his anger*): You must do better, Mollie. (*He screams.*) *True Animalism cannot tolerate selfishness.*

NAPOLEON Order, comrades, order! We must not get angry at meetings. We must always be reasonable.

SNOWBALL Let us pass on to more serious matters. Some of our weaker comrades seem unable to learn the seven commandments by heart.

BOXER (*confessing*): Yes.

SNOWBALL I have reduced the commandments to a single saying: 'Four Legs Good: Two Legs Bad'. This contains the essential principle of Animalism and whoever has thoroughly grasped it will be safe from human influences.

HEN I object. I have only two legs. So have all birds.

Protest breaks out among the BIRDS.

SNOWBALL (*silencing the din*): This is not so, comrades. A bird's wing is an organ of propulsion, not manipulation. It should therefore be regarded as a leg. The distinguishing mark of Man is the *hand,* the instrument with which he does all his mischief.

HEN I don't understand. Does that mean we are good?

SNOWBALL Yes, you are good.

HEN Good.

ANOTHER HEN But I've still only got two legs.

SNOWBALL It doesn't matter if you don't understand, as long as you accept my explanation. Do you accept my explanation?

CHICKENS Yes, we do. We accept your explanation.

SNOWBALL So repeat after me please:

Four legs good

Two legs bad.

The canon develops, sung by all the ANIMALS *as they learn the new maxim.*

ALL **Four legs good**

**Four legs good
Two legs bad
Two legs bad.**

The scene ends with the SHEEP *alone, still singing a joyful chorus. Having learnt it, they don't want to stop.*

Lights out.

BOY   The sheep enjoyed the song. They went on singing for fifteen minutes without stopping. Meanwhile Mr Jones was at the Red Lion every night complaining.

Lights up on the bar of the Red Lion. MR JONES *is talking to his neighbours.*

MR JONES   I think everybody should know – every man, every animal – the terrible wickedness that is now flourishing at Manor Farm. No, I won't call it 'Animal Farm'. They'd be starving if they didn't practise cannibalism. Do you know that they torture each other with red hot horse-shoes? Worst of all, they have their females in common . . . !

Lights out.

BOY   The other farmers were frightened by the rebellion at Animal Farm, and very anxious to stop their own animals hearing too much about it. But rumours of a wonderful farm – where the animals managed without human beings – continued to circulate. The pigs saw to that. They sent out flights of pigeons to mingle with the animals on neighbouring farms, tell them about the rebellion, and teach them the tune of 'Beasts of England'.

Lights up. The black figures manipulate flocks of pigeons on wires, swooping them round and round the stage. Meanwhile, 'Beasts of England' is heard in the distance. JONES *listens with two other* FARMERS.

JONES   How can the animals bring themselves to sing such contemptible rubbish! They need a good flogging.

BOY   And yet the song was irrepressible. The blackbirds whistled it in the hedges, the pigeons cooed it in the elms, it got into the din of the smithies and the tune of the church bells.

The sounds of the countryside are combined with 'Beasts of England'.

The human beings listened, and secretly trembled. For they heard in the song a prophecy of their future doom.

The FARMERS *look frightened as the lights fade. Early in October, the* ANIMALS *met their next great test. Lights up. The* PIGEONS *bring a message to* SNOWBALL. *He listens to them.*

SNOWBALL   Jones, Jones is coming!

BOY   The attack had long been expected, and everyone was prepared. Snowball had studied an old book of Julius Caesar's campaigns which he had found in the farmhouse. He gave his orders quickly and in a couple of minutes, every animal was at his post.

Martial music. JONES, *accompanied by the other* FARMERS, *opens the five barred gate. He leads the posse with a gun in his hands. The rest carry sticks.*

SNOWBALL   (*an order*): Retreat, retreat!

The ANIMALS *turn and run into the barn. The* MEN *give a shout of triumph.*

JONES   After them!

Once the MEN *are inside the barn, the* HORSES, *the* COWS, *and the rest of the* PIGS *who are not in the barn emerge from their hiding places and cut off their retreat. Then the* MEN *are driven out of the barn.*

SNOWBALL   Charge!!

SNOWBALL *charges straight for* JONES. JONES *raises his gun, and fires.* SNOWBALL *flattens himself for an instant before resuming his charge, and behind him a* SHEEP *drops dead.* SNOWBALL *charges* JONES' *legs.* JONES *is knocked over and his gun flies out of his hands.*

ANIMALS   Hooray!

BOXER *rears on his hind legs and strikes out with his great iron shod hoofs. His first blow knocks a* STABLE LAD *lifeless. At the sight, the* MEN *drop their sticks and start running. Panic spreads. The* MEN *are gored, kicked, beaten, trampled on. The* MEN *rush out of the yard, jump the gate, and make a dash for the main road. All this is enacted in great detail and accompanied by music.*

BOXER *paws with his hoof at the* STABLE LAD.

BOXER He is dead. I didn't mean to do that. I forgot that I was wearing iron shoes.

SNOWBALL No sentimentality, comrade! War is war. The only good human being is a dead human being!

BOXER I don't want to take life. Not even human life.

MURIEL *slowly pulls the flag up the flagpole. The* ANIMALS *lower their heads and sing 'The Green Flag' quietly.*

SQUEALER But see the banners of the grass are raised,
The trees are striding through the dawn.

The STABLE LAD, *unobserved, comes round and runs off.*

NAPOLEON Quickly! After him!

BOXER No. Let him go. He was only a lad.

There is an uneasy pause.

SQUEALER Comrades, we must commemorate this great day. Medals must be awarded.

MURIEL Medals?

SQUEALER I suggest 'Animal Hero First Class'.

NAPOLEON I propose that Boxer be named 'Animal Hero, First Class'.

ALL (*voting*): Agreed!

MURIEL Give Snowball a medal too.

The ANIMALS *look nervously at the dead* SHEEP.

SNOWBALL Our dear comrade here is also a hero. But alas, he is a dead hero.

SQUEALER Let us confer a decoration posthumously on him: 'Animal Hero, Second Class'.

ALL (*voting*): Agreed! Agreed!

MOLLIE *enters from the stables.*

MOLLIE Have they all gone?

SQUEALER Yes.

MOLLIE Is it safe?

SNOWBALL Yes.

MOLLIE I am sorry I couldn't stay. I had to hide my head in the hay. I can't stand explosions.

The ANIMALS *all look at her.*

SQUEALER Comrades, what shall we call this glorious day. Every October the twelfth, every anniversary we shall have a celebration. And what shall the battle be called?

BOXER There is only one name for the battle: Snowball's Battle.

NAPOLEON (*very quickly*): No. I think you will agree that that is the wrong name. You all fought this battle. You all brought us victory. Let it be named the Battle of the Cowshed. That was after all the place – the place where the ambush was sprung.

ALL Agreed! Agreed!

NAPOLEON *and* SNOWBALL *look at each other.*

Lights down.

BOY Now Winter drew on . . . .

Lights up. MOLLIE *and* CLOVER *are together.*

CLOVER Mollie, I have something very serious to say to you. This morning I saw you looking over the hedge that divides Animal Farm from Mr Pilkington's farm. Mr Pilkington was standing on the other side of the hedge. And – I was a long way away, but I am almost certain I saw this – he was talking to you, and you were allowing him to stroke your nose. What does that mean Mollie?

MOLLIE He didn't! I wasn't! It isn't true . . . . (*She begins to paw the ground.*)

CLOVER Mollie: Look me in the face. Do you give me your word of honour that Mr Pilkington was not stroking your nose?

MOLLIE How dare you ask me such questions?

MOLLIE *takes to her heels and gallops away. The lights fade.*

BOY Three days later, Mollie disappeared.

Lights up on all the ANIMALS *at the meeting.*

1ST PIGEON We have seen Mollie on the other side of the village. She was between the shafts of a smart dogcart painted red and black.

A vision of MOLLIE *appears trotting in an idyllic dappled light. She is covered with ribbons and is led by* MR PILKINGTON *who bears a whip. The* ANIMALS *stare in disbelief.*

2ND PIGEON Mr Pilkington was stroking her nose and feeding her sugar.

MOLLIE *sings as she trots.*

MOLLIE **Twenty-seven ribbons**
Twenty-seven ribbons
Sugar lumps for Mollie
A kindly blacksmith
And a gentle vet.
Master brought my ribbons
And my shiny brasses –
Give the humans what they want
And that is what you'll get.

And the wheels flow around
With a whirring, purring sound
As I step along Speedwell Lane,
And I hurry home to the curry-comb
With twenty-seven multi-coloured ribbons in
 my mane.

Twenty-seven ribbons

Sugar lumps for Mollie
A careful grooming
After every trip.
I have heard some horses
Say that Man is cruel –
But if you're obedient
You'll seldom feel the whip.

Yes the wheels flow around
With a whirring, purring sound
As I step along Speedwell Lane,
And I hurry home
To the curry-comb
With twenty-seven multi-coloured ribbons in
　　　my mane.
Twenty-seven ribbons
Twenty-seven ribbons
Twenty-seven ribbons in my mane.

MOLLIE *disappears.*

Lights down.

BOY　None of the animals ever mentioned Mollie again.

Lights up in the barn on all the ANIMALS.

By custom, it was now expected that the pigs should decide all questions of farm policy. But their decisions still had to be ratified by a majority vote. This arrangement would have worked well enough if it had not been for the continual disputes between Snowball and Napoleon.

SNOWBALL　I propose that we sow a bigger acreage with barley!

The ANIMALS *shout agreement and disagreement after each proposition. It is a very noisy meeting.*

NAPOLEON　I propose that we sow a bigger acreage with oats!

SNOWBALL　The big Copse Meadow is just right for cabbages!

NAPOLEON　The meadow is useless for anything except roots!

Uproar from the ANIMALS.

SNOWBALL　Comrades! Comrades!

BOY At the meetings, Snowball often won over the majority by his brilliant speeches . . . .

SNOWBALL **Yesterday had the smell of blood,**
Slavery, loss and pain.
Today is sweaty with constant work
And I know that you feel the strain.
But tomorrow, tomorrow is your children's day
And we labour so they may gain
The potatoes and apples and barley of the future
With its deep green meadows
And its towering golden grain –
Tomorrow.

ALL Tomorrow!

SNOWBALL We spend too much time, comrades, carting dung.

MURIEL *enters carrying a child's blackboard in her teeth. On it there is a map of the fields drawn in chalk.*

I ask you to support this scheme. Here is a map of the farm. Each animal is given a starting point, he moves three steps a day. If all animals drop their dung directly in the field, and at a different spot each day, the saving of labour in carting will . . .

NAPOLEON May I interrupt? I have no schemes, I believe in quiet, conscientious work, not risks.

BOY Napoleon was better at canvassing support for himself between the meetings. He was especially successful with the sheep, who were always ready to interrupt when Snowball's scheme sounded too difficult.

NAPOLEON Snowball's scheme may be very ingenious, but it won't work.

SNOWBALL Yes, it will work!

SHEEP (*a raucous interruption*):

Four legs good
Four legs good
Two legs bad
Two legs bad.

BOXER (*silencing them*): Now then, now then! The sheep must allow us to talk. We must say what we think.

NAPOLEON *turns and looks at* BOXER *and smiles.*

NAPOLEON Of course, Boxer.

Lights fade.

BOY But of all their controversies, the most bitter was the one over the windmill – the windmill designed by Snowball.

A large sheet of paper has been pinned over the barn entrance. On it, is a rough working drawing of a windmill. The ANIMALS *examine it with excitement and interest.* SNOWBALL *is not there.* NAPOLEON *looks at the drawing, sniffs it, and then lifts his leg and urinates on it.*
The ANIMALS *gasp.*

NAPOLEON (*calling*): Snowball!

SNOWBALL (*entering*): I'm here, comrade.

NAPOLEON This windmill of yours is impossible.

SNOWBALL Difficult, comrade, not impossible. We will have to gather stone for its walls, we will have to make sails, we will have to buy dynamos. I believe all this can be accomplished in one year.

NAPOLEON One year!

SNOWBALL It will supply our farm with electrical power.

NAPOLEON But we can't do everything at once! Why can't you be realistic?

NAPOLEON *stares at* SNOWBALL.

The rest of the ANIMALS *are uneasy.*

SNOWBALL I *am* being realistic. This power will do your work for you. You can graze at your ease in the fields or improve your minds with reading and conversations. So much labour will be saved that you animals will only need to work three days a week.

MURIEL (*admiringly*): Snowball, how did you think of this?

SNOWBALL   Mr Jones left an excellent book behind: *A Thousand Useful Things to do About the House.* It has taught me how to lay bricks and to understand electricity. So now I can build windmills!

BOXER   Put it to the vote! Put it to the vote!

NAPOLEON   We'll be past voting, comrades, when our stomachs are empty. I'm a plain pig, a practical pig, and I say this. The great need at the moment is to increase food production. If we waste time on windmills, we'll starve to death.

SNOWBALL   Do you deny my ideas?

NAPOLEON   (*suddenly shouting*): Yes, I deny your ideas.

BOY   The animals are furious. War was near. They no longer wanted to argue; they wanted to fight.

The ANIMALS *divide into two factions on opposite sides of the stage and confront each other.*

1ST FACTION   **A vote for Snowball means food for the future!**

2ND FACTION   **A vote for Napoleon and eat it now!**

1ST FACTION   **A vote for Snowball means food for the future!**

2ND FACTION   **A vote for Napoleon and eat it now!**

SNOWBALL*'s voice rises above the din.*

SNOWBALL   Think, comrades, how life can be on Animal Farm when sordid labour is lifted from our back. I am thinking far beyond chaff-cutters and turnip-slicers. Electricity can do many things. It can operate threshing machines, ploughs and harrows, rollers and reapers. And it can supply every stall with its own electric light, its own hot and cold water, *and* an electric heater.

As SNOWBALL *speaks, the* ANIMALS *in* NAPOLEON*'s faction change their minds and go over to* SNOWBALL*'s. Only the* PIGS *remain.*

Think of the future. Think of your children. Think of the dignity of animals when they are freed from toil. Do you vote for the windmill?

ALL   Yes, we do. We vote for the windmill.

Suddenly NAPOLEON *utters a high-pitched blood-curdling scream. There is a loud noise of dogs baying and the silhouettes of two enormous black* DOGS *appear in the barn behind the drawing of the windmill. With a yelp, they tear down the drawing and attack* SNOWBALL. *He confronts them for a moment in terror, and then runs away through the gate and out of the farm. He is pursued by the* DOGS. *The* ANIMALS *are terrified. They watch as* SNOWBALL *is chased away into the distance.*

Silence.

BOXER   Snowball's gone.

CLOVER   Gone?

SQUEALER   Yes, gone, gone back to the world of men where he belongs. Snowball, who we now see, was little better than a traitor and a coward.

BOXER   (*emphatically*): He wasn't.

CLOVER   He fought bravely at the Battle of the Cowshed.

SQUEALER   Only the guilty run away. And I believe the time will come when we shall discover that Snowball's part in the battle was much exaggerated. Do you still support Snowball, comrades? Snowball with his moonshine of windmills?

The DOGS *come bounding back and surround* NAPOLEON, *asking for approval.*

BOXER   Where do those dogs come from?

NAPOLEON   They are my puppies. I've brought them up to be big dogs.

BENJAMIN   They wag their tails at you just as their parents wagged their tails at Mr Jones.

NAPOLEON   That's right, Benjamin. They are well trained . . . . From now on the Sunday morning debates are cancelled. They are unnecessary and waste time. In future, all questions relating to the working of the farm will be settled by a special committee of pigs, presided over by me. We shall meet in private, and afterwards communicate our decisions to the rest of you. All you animals will still assemble on Sunday morning to sing 'The Green Flag' and of course to receive your orders for the week. But there will be no more debates.

MURIEL   No more debates?

CLOVER   (*tentatively*): If there's no debate, there's no Animal Farm.

BOXER   Shan't we vote any more?

NAPOLEON   No, Boxer. But your wishes will be carefully considered by the special committee of the pigs. We live in dangerous times. We must show solidarity and have strong leadership. We must defend ourselves from our enemies.

SQUEALER   I'm sure Comrade Napoleon would be only too happy to let you make your own decisions by yourselves, but sometimes you might make the wrong decisions and then where should we be?

BOXER   That's right.

SQUEALER   Discipline, comrades, iron discipline, that is the watch-word for today. One false step, and our enemies will be upon us. Surely, comrades, you don't want Jones back?

BOY   Once again, this argument was unanswerable.

ANIMALS   No. We don't want Jones back.

BENJAMIN   But why can't we vote?

SQUEALER   Comrades. I trust every animal here appreciates the sacrifice that Comrade Napoleon has made in taking this extra labour upon himself. Do not imagine, comrades, that leadership is pleasure! On the contrary, it is a deep and heavy responsibility.

MURIEL   If having debates on Sunday mornings will bring Jones back, then the debates must stop.

SQUEALER   Perhaps the farmers will get to hear of our disagreements and think we are weak.

BOXER (*his mind made up*): Comrades. I have now had time to think things over and I think I have a solution. What Comrade Napoleon is offering us is leadership. He is a practical pig, a pig of few words. Let's do what he says. (*Pause.*) Agreed?

ALL (*voting*): Agreed! Agreed!

NAPOLEON Thank you, comrades.

NAPOLEON *and the* PIGS *leave. There is a long silence. The* ANIMALS *look at* BOXER.

BOXER (*reassuringly*): We have chosen wisely, comrades. Napoleon is always right. **Long Live Animal Farm!**

ALL **Long Live Animal Farm!**

ACT TWO

The ANIMALS *are seen in a long line, waiting to pay their respects to the skull of* OLD MAJOR, *which is now nailed to the telegraph pole.*

BOY Every Sunday morning at ten o'clock, the animals assembled to pay their respects to Old Major. His skull, now clean of flesh, had been disinterred from the orchard and nailed to a telegraph pole.

SQUEALER And now Minimus, the first Animalist poet, will pay his tribute to Old Major.

MINIMUS Once all us animals' eyes were blind
To the fact of our slavery.
Old Major had a very clever mind,
He showed us Man's knavery.

Old Major
Please feed us!
Help us win our daily war.
Old Major
Please lead us!
Thank you very much, great boar!

So let us salute the skull of Major then.
O behold his enormous brains!
And every Sunday when the clock strikes ten
We'll march past his remains.

NAPOLEON I have a brief announcement, comrades. We must look to the future. Animalism will lead us to incredible achievements. No task is too great for Animalism. *We're going to build a windmill!*

ALL What?

NAPOLEON The special committee of pigs expects that the building of the windmill will take two years.

NAPOLEON *leaves.*

BOXER But I thought that Napoleon thought that the windmill . . . ?

SQUEALER Napoleon was never actually opposed to the

windmill. The plan which Snowball drew was
copied from some papers stolen from Napoleon. The
windmill is actually Napoleon's own creation. And it
always was.

BENJAMIN Then why did he speak so strongly against it?

SQUEALER That was Comrade Napoleon's cunning. He seemed
to oppose the windmill simply as manoeuvre to get
rid of Snowball. This is something called tactics.
Napoleon is expert at tactics.

MURIEL But why did he want to get rid of Snowball?

SQUEALER Because he was not practical, comrades, not realistic.
He went too fast. I suppose you could say he was
leading us quickly to starvation. The windmill will
prevent that.

BOXER (*his mind made up*): If Comrade Napoleon says we
need a windmill, then we must build a windmill.
Agreed?

ALL (*voting*): Agreed! Agreed!

SQUEALER Thank you, comrades.

BOY But the windmill proved difficult, because there
were no stones on the farm. There were some huge
boulders on top of a cliff. But the problem was how
to break the boulders into pieces the right size. After
weeks of thought . . .

SQUEALER (*an inspiration*): Ah!

BOY The pigs had an idea.

SQUEALER We will shove these huge boulders over the edge of
the cliff. We will smash them by using the force of
gravity.

Lights up. Music.
BOXER *is seen trying to push the boulder. During the
song the other* ANIMALS *come and help him.*

BOXER **There was a whacking great limestone boulder**
Must've weighed near a ton.
I tried to shift it with my shoulder –
Ugh! (*Shoving.*)

                        – Couldn't be done.
                        So I called a passing comrade over
                        And she came at the run.

BOXER & CLOVER: We tried to move that limestone boulder
                        Ugh! (*Shoving.*)
                        – Couldn't be done.
                        We appealed to the Sheep Committee
                        Called up the Goats' Brigade
                        And the chickens and the geese to shift that rock –
                        Ugh! (*Shoving.*)

ALL   – But it just stayed.
                        It just stayed where it was
                        That great lump of stone
                        And all of the beasts
                        Gave a mighty moan
                        We'll never shift it!
                        The rock's too big!

SQUEALER   Give it one more try!

MINIMUS   Says a stout-hearted pig!

ALL   So we gave one more shove
                        And we gave one more lift
                        And that whacking great boulder
                        Started to shift
                        And we gave it a shove
                        With all our heart and soul
                        And that whacking great boulder
                        Started to roll – and roll – and roll and –

                        The ANIMALS *pause as they watch the boulder roll over
                        the edge. There is a huge crash.*

ALL   There was a whacking great limestone boulder
                        But the animals worked as one
                        Yes, through animal co-operation
                        Anything can be done!
                        Anything can be done!
                        Anything can be done!

CLOVER   Boxer! Don't over-strain yourself.

BOXER   We're not getting enough food. I'll pick up when

the spring grass comes on.

CLOVER　I am worried about you, Boxer. You think there are two answers to every problem: 'I will work harder'; or 'Napoleon is always right'.

BOXER　They *are* the answers.

L*ights down.*

BOY　All that year the animals worked like slaves to till the fields. They also worked to build the windmill.

Lights up. The ANIMALS *are seen building the windmill.*

But they were happy in their work. Everything they did was for their own benefit and for those who would come after them, not for a pack of idle, thieving human beings.

NAPOLEON　(*entering*): Comrades, in future there will be work on Sunday afternoons. This work is of course strictly voluntary. But any animal who absents himself from it must expect to have his rations reduced by half. Furthermore, I have decided on a new policy. From now on, Animal Farm will engage in trade with neighbouring farms.

MURIEL　Comrade Napoleon, will you repeat that?

NAPOLEON　Animal Farm will engage in trade with neighbouring farms!

The ANIMALS *gasp in amazement. The* DOGS *growl.*

This is, of course, not for any commercial purpose. We need money to buy the materials which are urgently necessary – tools, paraffin oil, string. And dog biscuits. I am therefore making arrangements to sell a stack of hay and part of our current wheat crop. If we need more money later, to buy a dynamo for the windmill for instance, it will have to be obtained by the sale of eggs. There is always a market for eggs in the village.

The HENS *cluck in protest.*

HEN　What! What! What about our chicks?

The DOGS *growl.*

NAPOLEON   The hens should welcome this sacrifice as their own special contribution towards the building of the windmill.

The ANIMALS *are uneasy. Two young* PIGS *come forward.*

1ST PIG   Comrade Leader, we represent the younger pigs and we must object. These were among the earliest resolutions passed after Jones was expelled.

2ND PIG   One:

1ST PIG   Never to have any dealings with human beings.

2ND PIG   Two:

3RD PIG   Never to engage in trade.

2ND PIG   Three:

1ST PIG   Never to make use of money.

SQUEALER   Are you certain this isn't something you have dreamed, comrade? Have you any record of these resolutions? Are they written down anywhere?

BENJAMIN   I remember them.

CLOVER   We all remember them.

BOXER   Comrade Snowball always told us not to behave like men.

ALL   Yes, that's right.

SHEEP   (*interrupting*): **Four legs good**
Four legs good
Two legs bad
Two legs bad

NAPOLEON *raises his trotter for silence.*

NAPOLEON   There is no need for any further discussion. I have recognised necessity. We need money – so we will engage in trade. I have made all the arrangements. There will be no need for any of you animals to come into contact with human beings – that would clearly be most undesirable. I shall do that myself. Mr Whymper, a solicitor living in the village, has agreed to act as the agent between Animal Farm and the outside world. He will visit the farm every Monday morning to receive his instructions.

An uneasy silence.

Long live Animal Farm!

ALL Long live Animal Farm.

A bicycle bell is heard ringing.

BOY Every Monday, Mr Whymper visited the farm.

MR WHYMPER *rides in on a bicycle, dismounts and shakes hands with* NAPOLEON.

The animals watched him with dread. Nevertheless, the sight of Napoleon on all fours, delivering orders to Whymper, who stood on two legs, roused their pride and partly reconciled them to the new arrangement.

NAPOLEON Do I make myself clear?

WHYMPER Perfectly, Mr Napoleon.

MR WHYMPER *hands a cheque to* NAPOLEON.

NAPOLEON Cheques are no use to me. I need five pound notes.

The ANIMALS *watch in delight as* MR WHYMPER *counts out the five pound notes.*

WHYMPER One, Two, Three, Four, Five, Six, Seven, Eight, Nine, Ten.

NAPOLEON That makes fifty pounds.

ANIMALS (*in wonder*): Fifty pounds!

NAPOLEON Thank you, Mr Whymper.

WHYMPER It's been a real pleasure, Mr Napoleon.

NAPOLEON *and the* ANIMALS *watch* MR WHYMPER *ride off on his bicycle. Suddenly* NAPOLEON *leads all the* PIGS *into the farmhouse at a fast trot.*

BOY It was about this time that the pigs suddenly moved into the farmhouse.

BOXER Why are they going in there?

SQUEALER (*at the farmhouse door*): It is absolutely necessary that the pigs, who are after all the brains of the farm, should have a quiet place to work in. It is also more suited to the dignity of the Leader to live in a house than a mere sty.

He leaves. The lights change.

1ST SHEEP (*gossiping*): I hear that the pigs take their meals in the kitchen.

2ND SHEEP And use the drawing room to play in.

3RD SHEEP And sleep in the beds.

4TH SHEEP Never!

BOXER (*keeping order*): Napoleon is always right.

CLOVER I remember a definite ruling against beds.

MURIEL *and* CLOVER *go over to the barn and look at the seven commandments on the wall.*

CLOVER Muriel, read me the fourth commandment.

MURIEL (*reading with some difficulty*): It says: 'Animals shall never sleep in beds with sheets on'.

CLOVER I don't remember the fourth commandment mentioning sheets.

MURIEL But it must have done. It's there on the wall.

SQUEALER *looks out of the upstairs window of the farmhouse.*

SQUEALER Comrades! You did not suppose, surely comrade, that there was ever a ruling against *beds?* A bed merely means a place to sleep in. A pile of straw in a stall is a bed, properly regarded. The rule was against *sheets*, which are a human invention. We have removed the sheets from the farmhouse beds and sleep between blankets. And very comfortable blankets they are too.

Lights down.

BOY By the autumn, the animals were tired but happy. They had had a hard year and after selling part of the hay and corn to Mr Whymper, they were still hungry. But the windmill compensated for everything.

Music. Lights up on all the ANIMALS *building the windmill, block by block.*

BOXER We are working harder. We are building our windmill.

ALL Hooray!

BOY Only Old Benjamin refused to grow enthusiastic.

BENJAMIN Huh! Windmills! Electricity! The more you have the more you want. God has given me a tail to keep the flies off. But I'd sooner have no tail and no flies.

The lights change. It is winter. Snow falls. The ANIMALS *huddle in a group.*

BOY In January food fell short. For days at a time, the animals had nothing to eat but chaff and mangels.

ALL Food! Where's our food? Give us food!

CLOVER Have you heard what the pigeons are saying? When we're really weak, Jones intends to bring twenty men against us all armed with guns.

BOY Starvation stared them in the face. But it was vitally necessary to hide this face from the outside world.

The lights change. NAPOLEON *and* MR WHYMPER *enter from the barn.* MR WHYMPER *is once more counting out the money.*

WHYMPER One, two, three, four, five, six, seven, eight, nine, ten. Another fifty pounds for your very fine grain, Mr Napoleon.

NAPOLEON Thank you, Mr Whymper.

WHYMPER I hear rumours in the village that you're running short of food.

NAPOLEON Not so, Mr Whymper.

WHYMPER Won't you sell me some more grain then, Mr Napoleon?

NAPOLEON No. The animals must be fed, and fed well. Goodbye, Mr Whymper.

WHYMPER Very well. Cheerio, Mr Napoleon.

MR WHYMPER *rides off on his bicycle.*

BOY   Mr Whymper has been nicely fooled. The grain bins
had been filled at Napoleon's order with sand,
which was then covered with what was left of the
grain. In fact, the animals were desperately hungry.

Lights up on the Sunday morning meeting. NAPOLEON
is absent. SQUEALER *is speaking.*

SQUEALER   Comrades. We need grain. Napoleon has therefore
decreed that the hens must surrender their eggs.

HENS   (*screaming in protest*): What?

High up on a rafter, all the HENS *appear. They are
sitting out of reach.*

SQUEALER   He has accepted, through the good offices of
Whymper, a contract for four hundred eggs a week.
The price of these will pay for enough grain and
meal to give us food until Summer.

1ST HEN   But the clutches are ready for the spring sitting.

2ND HEN   It's murder if you take the eggs away now.

BOY   And for the first time since the expulsion of Jones,
there was something resembling a rebellion.

HENS   **We can't spare the eggs.**

SQUEALER   **You must do your duty.**

HENS   **We can't spare the eggs.**
Can't you see we're broody?

SQUEALER   **We must have the eggs**
We must pay our way now.

HENS   **It's murder, yes murder**
To take our eggs away now.

SQUEALER   **Consider economics –**
The eggs have got to go.

HENS   **Consider our unborn chicks.**

SQUEALER   **We must have the eggs.**

HENS   **No! No!**
Till each egg has the right

To become a hen
There'll be no more eggs
To be sold to men,
There'll be no eggs at all.
Let the eggs rain down
From the henhouse sky.

The HENS *drop their eggs onto the* ANIMALS *below them.*

Let the egg yolks dry.
Till each egg has the right
To become a hen
There'll be no more eggs
To be sold to men.
There'll be no eggs at all.

NAPOLEON   (*entering*): **Our feathered comrades, it appears,**
Have lost all sense of reason
And their reactionary acts
Are tantamount to treason

To turn them back to sanity
And save them from self slaughter
I order that the hens shall be
Deprived of food and water.

BOY   For five days the hens held out.

HENS   (*weakening*): **Till each egg has the right**
To become a hen
There'll be no eggs at all.
Let the eggs rain down
From the henhouse sky.

The HENS *fall dead off the rafters, one by one.*

Let the eggshells smash
Let the good yolks dry.

Lights down.

BOY   Finally, they capitulated and went back to their
nesting boxes. Nine hens had died. (*A small toy van
crosses the stage to the gate and stops.*) From now on,
a grocer's van drove up to the farm once a

week to take the eggs away. And once a week the animals watched them go. But they still had no more to eat. (*The van leaves the stage.*) There was secret whispering in the night, a whispering that Napoleon, like Snowball, was soon to be chased away. Who was to chase him? Where was Mr Whymper's money going? Why was there no food? Morale was very low. Napoleon knew that he had to do something.

NAPOLEON Comrades, I have alarming news. Snowball is secretly frequenting the farm by night!

The ANIMALS *quickly grow hysterical with fear.*

He has stolen the corn, upset the milk, broken the eggs, trampled the seedbeds, gnawed the bark off the fruit trees. Did you notice that window that was broken last week? Did you notice the drain of the cowshed? It was blocked up. I will go further. I believe that the lost key of the store shed was filched by Snowball and thrown down the well! Any animal who can give evidence of Snowball's villanies will be rewarded with extra rations.

ALL Extra rations!

Two COWS *come forward.*

COWS We have a unanimous statement to make. Snowball has crept into our stall and milked us in our sleep. All of us. Yes, all of us.

NAPOLEON There must obviously be a full investigation into Snowball's activities. (*Giving several deep sniffs.*) Snowball! He has been here! I can smell him distinctly!

The DOGS *let out bloodcurdling growls.* NAPOLEON *leaves accompanied by his dogs. The* ANIMALS *are very alarmed.*

BOY The animals were thoroughly frightened. It seemed to them that Snowball was an invisible influence who was everywhere.

SQUEALER *enters suddenly. The* ANIMALS *jump with fear.*

SQUEALER Comrades! The most terrible thing has been discovered. We had thought that Snowball's opposition to Comrade Napoleon was caused by his vanity and ambition. But we were wrong, comrades. Snowball was in league with Jones from the very start. He was Jones' secret agent all the time. This has been proved by documents which have only just been discovered. To my mind, this explains a great deal, comrades. Did we not see for ourselves how he attempted to get us defeated and destroyed at the Battle of the Cowshed!

There is a stunned silence.

BOXER He didn't. Snowball fought bravely at the Battle of the Cowshed. I saw him myself.

MURIEL We made him Animal Hero, First Class, immediately afterwards.

SQUEALER That was our mistake, comrades. For we now know that in reality he was trying to lure us to our doom. Do you not remember how Snowball suddenly turned and fled, and many animals followed him? Surely you remember that, comrades?

The ANIMALS *are confused.*

CLOVER I remember that Snowball turned and retreated.

MURIEL But that was his tactics. Military tactics.

BOXER Comrade Squealer, I do not believe that Comrade Snowball was a traitor at the beginning. What he has done since is different. But I believe that at the Battle of the Cowshed, he was a good comrade.

SQUEALER Our Leader, Comrade Napoleon, has stated categorically – *categorically*, comrades – that Snowball was Jones' agent from the very beginning. Yes, and from long before the rebellion was ever thought of!

A long pause. The ANIMALS *look confused. They watch* BOXER.

BOXER   Comrade Napoleon says that?

SQUEALER Yes, he does.

BOXER   Then that is different. If Comrade Napoleon says it, it must be right.

SQUEALER (*delighted*): There you are, comrades! There you see the true spirit of Animalism!

There is a roar of rage from NAPOLEON. *He appears at the window of the farmhouse.*

NAPOLEON Comrades! We have been robbed! When I capture Whymper, he shall be boiled in oil and then torn apart by every pig on the farm. The five pound notes are forgeries. Whymper has got the eggs for nothing! Death to Whymper!

ALL   (*hysterical again*): Death to Whymper! Death to Whymper!

SQUEALER Let me give you a warning. Every animal on this farm must keep his eyes very wide open. We know that some of you are Snowball's secret agents. We know you are! We have sniffed you out. And we will hunt you down.

The ANIMALS *look uneasily at each other as the lights fade.*

BOY   Four days later, Napoleon ordered all the animals to assemble.

Lights up. Enter NAPOLEON *and* SQUEALER.

NAPOLEON Comrades. There is a terrible threat to our future. There are traitors here on Animal Farm. The traitors must be brought to justice.

SQUEALER Bring them before us. Let the trials commence.

Two young PIGS *enter to be tried.*

1ST PIG We represent the younger pigs.

NAPOLEON Confess your crimes.

A silence.

1ST PIG What?

NAPOLEON Confess your crimes!

1ST PIG (*anxiously starting to play his part*): Oh yes, we have been secretly in touch with Snowball.

2ND PIG Ever since his expulsion.

1ST PIG We collaborated with him.

2ND PIG And we have entered into an agreement with him to hand over Animal Farm to Mr Jones.

NAPOLEON What has Snowball admitted to you?

1ST PIG That he has been Jones' secret agent for many years.

NAPOLEON shrieks. The barn door opens and the DOGS begin to drag the PIGS inside.

NAPOLEON It saddens me that the younger pigs should be guilty of such treason.

1ST PIG You told us . . . We would live . . . If we confessed!

The doors shut on the PIGS. They shriek as they are bitten to death. NAPOLEON looks at the ANIMALS.

NAPOLEON Has any other animal anything to confess?

Two HENS enter to be tried.

SQUEALER Confess!

1ST HEN Snowball appeared to me in a dream and incited me to disobey Napoleon's orders.

2ND HEN We led the rebellion over the eggs. We fully confess our faults.

NAPOLEON shrieks. The HENS are dragged into the barn and killed.
A silence.
A BULL comes forward nervously to be tried.

SQUEALER Next! Confess!

BULL I confess to having hidden six turnips during last year's harvest. I have eaten them one by one in secret. Night after night.

NAPOLEON shrieks. The BULL is dragged into the barn and killed.
Lights down.

BOY   The air was heavy with the smell of blood –
       unknown since the days of Jones. But this seemed
       far worse. Until today, no animal had killed another
       animal. Not even a rat had been killed.

       Lights up. The ANIMALS *are standing round a big pool
       of blood on the floor. A long pause.*

CLOVER   What are you going to do, Boxer?

BOXER   I do not understand it. I would not have believed it.
         The only solution, as I see it, is to work harder.
         From now on, I shall get up a full hour earlier in the
         mornings. And work.

         BOXER *leaves.*

ALL   **Say what you think**
       But the best thing to think
       Is nothing –
       That's excellent thinking.

       Eat what you like
       But the best food to like
       Is nothing –
       It's not on the ration.

       Do what you want
       But the best thing to do
       Is nothing –
       And mind how you do it.

       Go where you want
       But the place to go
       Is nowhere –
       You might get permission.

       Obey them.
       When they tell you what to do.
       You are nothing.
       Nothing.

       Believe them
       When they tell you what is true.
       You're nothing.
       Nothing.

**Keep your nose to the grindstone
And your shoulder to the wheel.
Listen
When they tell you what to feel
And –**

**Feel what you like
But the best thing to feel
Is nothing**

(*Whispering:*)
Nothing.

CLOVER, BENJAMIN *and* MURIEL *are by the barn.*

CLOVER Read the sixth commandment please, Benjamin.

BENJAMIN I refuse to meddle in such matters.

CLOVER Will you read it, Muriel?

MURIEL 'Animals shall never kill animals without good cause'.

CLOVER I don't remember those last three words, 'without good cause'.

MURIEL The commandment has not been violated. There was good reason to kill any animal who helped Snowball.

CLOVER (*with determination*): We must start again. We must try to remember what Old Major said and start again. Beasts of England, Beasts of Ireland Beasts of land and sea and skies.

SQUEALER Comrades, by a special decree of Comrade Napoleon, 'Beasts of England' has been abolished. From now on it is forbidden to sing it.

CLOVER Why?

SQUEALER It is no longer needed, comrade, that's why. 'Beasts of England' expressed our longing for a better society in the days to come. But now the days to come have come. That society has been established. Clearly the song no longer has any purpose.

CLOVER Do you agree? I want to know.

MURIEL   Yes.

Lights change. MINIMUS *is singing the new anthem.*

MINIMUS   **But see! The trotters of the pigs are raised!**
The swine advance with bellies stout!
And the green flag is flying
With the curly tail and snout!
Yes, pigs are leading all the animals.
Oh, follow them, nor reason why,
For the green flag is flying
And all England is our sty
Is our sty, is our sty, is our sty!

BOXER   Somehow or other, that song doesn't seem to come up to 'Beasts of –

ALL   Sshh!!

BOXER   – to what we used to sing.

Lights fade.

BOY   As the summer wore on, the rumours of an impending attack grew stronger and stronger. It was harvest time. It was inexplicable that there was no food. It was also inexplicable that Mr Whymper was visiting the farm again. In fact, all the grain was being secretly sold to him for ready cash so that the pigs could buy whisky.

Lights up. SQUEALER *dances in and addresses the animals.*

SQUEALER   **Animalism is a complicated business**
Inflexible equality is unrealistic
Our system's successful, though with
Certain contradictions
The proof is in the pudding
Let me quote you statistics.

The production of every class of foodstuff has increased. Some by two hundred percent, some by three hundred percent, some by five hundred percent. As the case might be. Isn't this a great achievement?

BENJAMIN   We're still hungry.

SQUEALER   What? Speak up Benjamin. Let us hear your thoughts.

BENJAMIN   I have no thoughts.

SQUEALER   Then look happy. Do you never laugh, Benjamin?

BENJAMIN   I see nothing to laugh about.

SQUEALER   But we want you to laugh, Benjamin. All of us.
Come on. Laugh!

The DOGS *growl.* BENJAMIN *begins to laugh, his hysteria
mounting until he is completely out of control. The
other* ANIMALS *gather round him in sympathy. He
stops, broken.*

SQUEALER   Next time, Benjamin, laugh when I tell you to.

Lights down.

BOY   In September, by a tremendous effort – the windmill
was finished.

Lights up on the finished windmill. BOXER *pushes the
sails and they start to turn.*

ALL   Hooray!

NAPOLEON   May I personally congratulate each and every animal
on this achievement. The mill will be called
'Napoleon Mill'.

SQUEALER   Hip hip –

ALL   Hooray.

SQUEALER   Hip hip –

ALL   Hooray.

SQUEALER   Hip hip –

ALL   Hooray.

MINIMUS   (*entering in great excitement*): Comrades, comrades,
comrades!

I have a new poem. It is an ode to our father,
Comrade Napoleon. It is entitled Comrade Napoleon.

**Friend of the fatherless!
Fountain of happiness!
Lord of the swill bucket!**

> **Oh, how my soul is on**
> **Fire when I gaze at thy**
> **Calm and commanding eye**
> **Like the sun in the sky**
> **Comrade Napoleon!**
> **Comrade Napoleon!**
> **Comrade Napole-ole-ole-ole-on!**

NAPOLEON I approve of this poem.

MINIMUS (*turning a somersault*): Yippee!

NAPOLEON Such loyal sentiments are more than welcome in these treacherous times. I will reward you by appointing you my first Taster.

MINIMUS What do I have to taste?

NAPOLEON You will have the First Taste of every meal served to me. In case my enemies have poisoned it.

The lights change.

BOY Early in the new year Animal Farm was proclaimed a Republic.

NAPOLEON The president, who was elected unanimously, is me.

ALL Comrade Napoleon!
Comrade Napoleon!
Comrade Napole-ole-ole-ole-on!

The PIGS *leave. Lights change.*

BOY That night, the sound of loud singing came from the farmhouse . . .

PIGS (*drunk offstage*): Beasts of England, seize the prizes, Wheat and barley, oats and hay!

BOY The pigs had for some time been using all the money to buy more and more whisky. At about half-past-nine, Napoleon, wearing Mr Jones' old bowler hat, galloped out of the house.

NAPOLEON **On the dusty day when I was born**
I was not very big.
In fact, of a litter of seventeen,
I was the smallest pig.
It was more of a scramble than a birthday

And I came out back to front.
I was the last of the bunch
When it came to lunch
Yes, I was the litter's runt.

But a runt has to fight
For his share of the milk
If he fancies staying alive.
He'll kick with his feet
And cling to the teat
And the runt may yet survive.

And if that young runt
Grabs enough of the swill
Then his bite will be worse than his grunt.
He'll grow stately and stout
With an eloquent snout
But he knows he was the runt.

(His megalomania increases.)

And the runt seizes power
For he knows all the tricks –
Those he bites will never bite back.
And the piglet who once
Was the weakest of runts
Shall be leader of the pack.
Shall be the leader
Shall be the leader
Shall be the leader.

I have created a new decoration: The Order of the Green Banner. I have conferred it on myself.

Lights down.

BOY   And the very next morning, the attack came. The animals awoke to find that the men had surrounded the windmill in the night. It was clear they intended to blow it up.

Lights up.
The ANIMALS *look nervously at the distant windmill. It is surrounded by* MEN. *One is poised over an explosive plunger.*

NAPOLEON (*rallying them*): It's impossible! We have built the
walls far too thick for that. Courage, comrades!

The plunger is driven home. A huge explosion. All the
ANIMALS *fling themselves flat on the ground. The*
windmill is in ruins.

BOY Without waiting for any orders, the animals charged.

ALL Charge!

BOY They chased the men over the fields and off the
farm.

The ANIMALS *stand among the ruins of the windmill.*

BOXER Our windmill is gone. Even the foundations are
destroyed.

CLOVER It's as though it had never been.

PIGS Hooray!

BOXER (*amazed*): Why are you cheering?

SQUEALER To celebrate our victory!

BOXER What victory!

SQUEALER What victory, comrade? Have we not driven the
enemy off our soil, the sacred soil of Animal
Farm?

BOXER But they've destroyed our windmill. And we have
worked on it for two years!

SQUEALER What does it matter? We will build another
windmill.

MINIMUS And another windmill.

SQUEALER We will build six windmills if we feel like it. You do
not appreciate, comrade, the mighty thing that we
have done. The enemy was in occupation of this
very ground that we stand upon. And now – thanks
to the leadership of Comrade Napoleon – we have
won every inch of it back again.

BOXER Then we have won back what we already had.

SQUEALER Yes. That is our victory.

NAPOLEON *appears at the window.*

NAPOLEON On this day of joy, you must hear the other good news. There is now no more fear on Animal Farm. The traitor Snowball has been eliminated. One of our comrades, a Bull, who I will not name for reasons of security, is enslaved on the farm where Snowball has been wallowing in luxury. This hero broke into Snowball's sty and gored him to death. Snowball is no more! You need be frightened no longer.

MINIMUS I shall write a poem about it!

NAPOLEON Excellent!

The PIGS *exit.*

BOXER For the first time, it occurs to me that I am getting old.

CLOVER A horse's lungs do not last forever.

BOXER They'll keep me going long enough to see the windmill rebuilt.

Lights change. The ANIMALS *begin to rebuild the windmill.*

ALL **There was a whacking great limestone boulder**
But the animals worked as one.
Yes, through animal cooperation
Anything can be done!
Anything can be done!
Anything can be done!

During the song, BOXER *collapses on the floor. The* ANIMALS *gather round.*

CLOVER Boxer! What is it?

BOXER It's my lung. It doesn't matter. I think you'll be able to finish the windmill now without me. There is a pretty good store of stone.

Enter SQUEALER.

SQUEALER (*full of concern*): Comrade Napoleon has learned with the deepest distress of this misfortune to one of the most loyal workers on the farm. He is already making arrangements to send Boxer to be treated in the village hospital.

CLOVER Why? I don't like animals leaving the farm.

BENJAMIN And I don't like to think of a sick comrade in the hands of human beings.

SQUEALER The veterinary surgeon in the village can treat Boxer's case more satisfactorily. It is the best thing for him.
BOXER begins to struggle to his feet, helped by the other ANIMALS. He reaches a kneeling position.

BOXER **I will be well, friends,**
And I'll retire, friends,
To the shadow of the chestnut tree
With time for thinking
And time for learning
The remainder of my ABC –
Um . . . D.

He struggles to his feet. Lights fade.

BOY The next day, a van arrived to take Boxer away.

Lights up on a MAN shutting the rear door of a horse-drawn van. He begins to lead the HORSE out of the gate.

CLOVER Goodbye, Boxer.

ALL (*quietly*): Goodbye, Boxer! Goodbye!

BENJAMIN comes running in braying at the top of his voice.

BENJAMIN Fools! Fools! Can't you see what is written on the side of that van.

MURIEL begins to spell out the words.

MURIEL Alfred Simmonds, Horse S L . . . . . . er, Horse S L . . .

BENJAMIN Oh shut up! Let me read it. 'Alfred Simmonds, Horse Slaughterer and Glue Boiler'. They are taking Boxer to the knackers!

ALL Boxer!

Cries of horror from the ANIMALS.

CLOVER Boxer! Boxer! Get out! Get out quickly! They are taking you to your death!

ALL   Boxer!

CLOVER *pleads with the* HORSE *pulling the van.*

CLOVER   Comrade, don't take your brother to his death.

ALL   Boxer!

BOXER'*s face appears at the small window at the back of the van. He tries to kick his way out. The* MAN *whips the* HORSE *and the van moves down the road.*

BOY   In a few moments, the sound of drumming hoofs grew fainter and died away. Three days later, Squealer made an announcement.

Enter SQUEALER:

SQUEALER   It has come to my knowledge that a foolish and wicked rumour has been circulating. Some of you noticed that the van which took Boxer away was marked 'Horse Slaughterer', and have actually come to the conclusion that Boxer was being sent to the knackers. It is almost unbelievable that any animal should be so stupid. Surely, surely you know your beloved leader, Comrade Napoleon, better than that? The explanation is really very simple. The van had previously been the property of the knacker, and had been bought by the veterinary surgeon who had not yet painted the old name out. That was how the mistake arose.

CLOVER   (*weeping*): I am very relieved to hear it.

MURIEL   So am I.

SQUEALER   Our beloved Comrade Boxer is dead. He died in the village hospital in spite of receiving every attention a horse could have.

NAPOLEON *appears drunk at the window of the farmhouse.*

NAPOLEON   Comrades. It has not after all been possible to bring back our lamented Comrade's remains. In a few days time, we pigs intend to hold a memorial banquet in Boxer's honour. Whisky will be drunk to his memory.

SQUEALER I am happy to say that I was present during Boxer's last hours. It was the most affecting sight I have ever seen. 'Forward Comrades', he whispered. 'Forward in the name of the rebellion. Long live Animal Farm! Long live Comrade Napoleon! Napoleon is always right'.

NAPOLEON I believe those maxims are ones which every animal would do well to adopt as his own.

CLOVER Were those his last words?

SQUEALER They were.

NAPOLEON 'Napoleon is always right.'

All the ANIMALS *bow their heads in remembrance of* BOXER. *They sing quietly. The lights begin to fade.*

ALL **Napoleon is always right**
Always right, always right.
We will work harder,
We will work harder.

Lights change.

BOY Years passed. Seasons came and went. The short animal lives fled by. Jones was dead – he had died in a home for drunks in another part of the country. The farm was more prosperous now. The windmill had been successfully rebuilt at last.

The windmill is seen with its sails turning.

But it was not after all used for generating electrical power. It was hired out for milling corn to neighbouring farmers and brought in a great deal of money. But the luxuries which Snowball had once taught the animals to dream of – the stall with electric light and hot and cold water, the three-day week – well, they were no longer talked about.

NAPOLEON *enters, fat and in full regalia.*

Napoleon was now a mature boar of twenty-four stone. One day the four sows all littered simultaneously, producing thirty-one young pigs between them. As Napoleon was now the only boar left on the farm, it was easy to guess at their parentage. Once again all rations were reduced. Only the pigs and dogs ate well.

SHEEP   Food! Where's our food! Give us food!

BENJAMIN   However much things change, they always remain the same.

Lights up on the Sunday morning meeting. NAPOLEON *addresses the* ANIMALS.

NAPOLEON   **Armed to the teeth**
We march along
Bullets not barley
We need
Can't you hear the alarm?
We'll save our farm
Before we feed!

As NAPOLEON *finishes his song, a tractor driven by a* PIG, *with another* PIG *standing behind him with a rifle, processes round the farmyard. As it goes off, the rifle is fired in a salute. An answering fusillade of rifle shots is heard off-stage. A large banner with a picture of* NAPOLEON's *head is unfurled.* NAPOLEON *and the* PIGS *go off.*
There is a silence. The ANIMALS *are horrified.*

CLOVER   **This isn't what we wanted**
This isn't what we meant
When our great rebellion began.
We hoped to make a farm where
All animals were free
Of hunger, whips and man.

MURIEL   (*contradicting her*):
You must be strong to grow Animalism
Rake out the stones
Rip out the weeds.
We'll reap the harvest of Animalism
Marching wherever
Napoleon leads.

At least we work for ourselves. None of us goes

upon two legs. None of us calls another creature
Master. All Animals Are Equal.

Lights up on a line of PIGS *across the back of the
stage. They are all dressed in incongruous bits of
human clothing. Slowly they rise to their feet, and
walk unsteadily round the stage on two feet.*

CLOVER   I think the world has been turned upside down.

BENJAMIN   I shall protest. For the first time in my life I shall
protest. (*He confronts the* PIGS.) You pigs have gone
far enough.

SHEEP   **Four legs good**
Four legs good
Two legs better!
Two legs better!

The PIGS *join in the round and leave.*
The lights fade.
The stage is empty except for BENJAMIN *and* CLOVER.
They look at the wall at the end of the barn.

CLOVER   My sight is failing. The wall looks different. Muriel,
read what you see.

MURIEL   No, I won't. I will never read anything again.

CLOVER   Will you read it, Benjamin?

BENJAMIN   There's only one commandment now. And just this
once I'll break my rule and read it to you. 'All
animals are equal. But some animals are more equal
than others.'

Lights change.

BOY   A week later, in the afternoon, a number of human
visitors arrived at the farm.

A deputation of neighbouring FARMERS *enter. The* PIGS
*welcome the humans effusively. There is much
shaking of hands and trotters.*

BOY   The farmers were shown around and expressed
great admiration for everything they saw. Especially
the windmill.

FARMERS (*in approval*): Ah!

PILKINGTON   Gentlemen, there was a time when the existence of a farm owned and operated by pigs was somehow felt to be abnormal. But what do I and my friends find here today? Not only the most up to date methods, but a discipline and an order which should be an example to all farmers everywhere. I believe indeed that the lower animals on Animal Farm do more work and receive less food than any animals in the country.

NAPOLEON   I too am happy that the period of misunderstanding is at an end. For a long time, there were rumours – circulated I have reason to believe, by some malignant enemy – that there was something subversive and even revolutionary in the outlook of myself and my colleagues. Nothing could be further from the truth! Our sole wish, now and in the past, is to live at peace and in normal business relations with our neighbours.

Lights change.

BOY   That evening loud laughter and bursts of singing came from the farmhouse.

A long dinner table. The PIGS *and the* FARMERS *are at their after-dinner speeches.*

PILKINGTON   (*on his feet*): And in conclusion, may I say that we have learnt a great deal here today.

BOY   What could be happening in there, now that for the first time, animals and human beings were meeting on terms of equality? All the other animals crept to the dining room window and peered and listened.

The other ANIMALS *gather round the window.*

PILKINGTON   Between pigs and human beings, there is not, and there need not be, any clash of interests whatever. Our struggles and our difficulties are the same. Is not the labour problem the same everywhere? If you have your lower animals, we have our lower classes! (*He laughs.*) And now gentlemen, and

ladies, will you be upstanding? Gentlemen I give
you a toast: To the prosperity of Animal Farm.

PIGS & FARMERS   Animal Farm!

They all sit.

NAPOLEON   (r*ising*): I have only one criticism to make on Mr
Pilkington's excellent and neighbourly speech. He
referred throughout to 'Animal Farm'. Mr Pilkington
could of course not know – for I am announcing it
now for the first time – that the name Animal Farm
has been abolished. Henceforward, the farm is to be
known as Manor Farm. I believe that is its correct
and original name. Gentlemen, I give you the same
toast as before, but in a different form: To the
prosperity of Manor Farm.

PIGS & FARMERS   (*rising to toast*): Manor Farm!

PILKINGTON   More profit for fewer people!

SQUEALER   More power in fewer hands!

NAPOLEON   More control of beast and human!

1ST FARMER   Use every inch of land!

PILKINGTON   **I see the future**
Shine on me
And pictures
Of the times to be –

Where chickens hatch
Ten thousand eggs
And never need
To stretch their legs

NAPOLEON   **And sheep in crates**
May spend their days
And grow us wool
But never graze.

1ST FARMER   **I see the future**
Shine on me
And pictures
Of the times to be –

The silky mink
The fiery fox
Shall grow us fur
Inside a box

SQUEALER **And calves be born**
Grow up, give birth,
And die but never
Walk on earth.

ALL **I see the future**
Shine on me
And pictures
Of the times to be.
Where day and night
And heat and cold
And birth and death
Are all controlled
And profit rules
And all is calm
On England's grey
And modern farm.

And profit rules
And all is calm
On England's grey
And modern farm.

PILKINGTON Science is a wonderful thing. In order to produce more meat and clothing, we men are developing a pig that can grow wool!

PIGS (*enraged*): What?

They strike the MEN.

NAPOLEON We pigs are experimenting with a human being who will lay eggs.

HUMANS (*enraged*): What?

They strike the PIGS. *As each figure is hit, he moves slowly upstage, and once his back is to the audience, the mask is removed – whether* PIG *or* HUMAN. *The figure then turns round. For the first time, the naked human face is seen.*

Both PIGS *and* MEN *are now unmasked.*

BOY   The creatures outside looked from pig to man, and from man to pig, and from pig to man again. But already it was impossible to say which was which.

The figures continue to stare out front.
The lights begin to fade.
The BOY *closes the book, replaces it in the bookcase, and walks slowly off the stage.*
The lights fade to darkness.

QUESTIONS AND EXPLORATIONS

1 Keeping Track

The questions in this section are designed to help your
reading and understanding of the play. They may be used as
you read the play or afterwards, for discussion or for writing.
Some are developed and expanded in the *Explorations* section.

Act One

1 In what ways is Mr Jones an inadequate farmer?
2 What, precisely, does Old Major dream?
3 What are Snowball's chief characteristics?
4 Why are Moses's stories of such interest to the animals?
5 What actions do the animals take to mark the
   overthrow of Jones?
6 What are the seven principles of Animalism?
7 What are Boxer's guiding principles?
8 How does Squealer justify the pigs' consumption of the
   cows' milk?
9 Why does the Wild Comrades Re-education
   Committee fail?
10 In what ways do Napoleon's plans for Animal Farm
   differ from those of Snowball?
11 How do the other farmers respond to the rebellion?
12 How does Mollie behave before, during and after the
   rebellion?
13 Summarise the arguments for and against the building
   of the windmill?
14 How do Napoleon and Squealer justify the end of
   democratic debate?

Act Two

1 Why, according to Squealer, had Napoleon opposed the
   building of the windmill?

2 Why do the animals no longer think of their hard work as slavery?

3 How does Napoleon justify trade with neighbouring farms?

4 How does Squealer justify the pigs' move into the farmhouse?

5 Why are the hens' eggs sold to Whymper?

6 Why does Napoleon tell the animals that Snowball has been visiting the farm secretly?

7 What reasons are given by Squealer and Napoleon for the trials and deaths of the animals?

8 Why is 'Beasts of England' abolished? In what way is Minimus's new anthem different from it?

9 After the completion of the windmill in what three ways does Napoleon increase his personal prestige?

10 How does Squealer attempt to turn the destruction of the windmill into a victory for the animals?

11 In what ways do the pigs turn the death of Boxer to their advantage?

12 'Years passed. Seasons came and went.' In what ways is Animal Farm now very similar to Manor Farm?

13 What replaces the seven principles of Animalism?

14 Why does Pilkington approve of the way the pigs run the farm?

15 At the end of the play in what ways have men and pigs become indistinguishable from each other?

2 Explorations

The questions in this section are more detailed and rely on your having read the whole play. Some of the questions develop ideas from the *Keeping Track* section. Because they tend to be more detailed, they offer the opportunity to develop the ideas in written, oral or practical assignments. They require detailed knowledge of the play: where appropriate, use quotation to substantiate your answers.

A Characters

In answering any of these questions you need to show an understanding of the ideas and motivations of the main characters of the play.

1   Look closely at the speech and actions of Benjamin. What is his reaction to the revolution? What kind of human behaviour is Orwell satirising?
2   Which character do you most sympathise with? Why?
3   In exile Trotsky wrote the *History of the Revolution* from his own point of view. Write the *History of Animal Farm* which Snowball might have written after he was cast out.
4   Write Napoleon's letter to Pilkington in which he reviews the success of the farm and invites Pilkington to make his visit at the end of Act 2. Write Pilkington's reply which he sends after the visit and the fight.
5   'In the Hot Seat'. Choose any one of the principle characters and write the transcript of a TV or radio programme in which he is interviewed about his behaviour.
6   Write a page of the local newspaper, *The Willingdon Gazette*, at the time of the rebellion. As well as a factual account of events it should include an interview with one of the principle characters, editorial comment and a letter from Mr Jones, complaining about the rebellion, stating his own innocence and asking for support to regain his farm.
7   The cat, Mollie and the Raven all reject the rebellion in various ways. What are their reasons for doing so and what kind of human attitudes do they each represent?
8   In what ways do Snowball and Napoleon represent different points of view?
9   Imagine that, following the events portrayed in the play, 'Manor Farm' is opened to the public. Write a brochure which Squealer produces to advertise the attractions of

the farm and guide a visitor round its principle sights.

10 *The Selected Works* by Minimus, the poet. Write a song or poem in the style of Minimus. It could praise the achievements of Napoleon and the pigs or re-write history, for example presenting an idealised account of Boxer's life. (You could try setting it to music, or writing words which would fit a popular tune.)

11 What are the characteristics of the pigs? Do they have any redeeming features?

B Themes

1 Why, by the end of the play, does the rebellion at Manor Farm fail? What could any of the animals have done to prevent this failure?

2 Translate the Seven Commandments, the principles of Animalism, into principles of human behaviour. If our society observed these commandments in what ways would we be advantaged or disadvantaged? What other commandments do you think we would need in order to create a perfect society?

3 Rewrite Old Major's dream to make it appropriate for the present day. In this updated vision you will need to imagine solutions to the central problems which appear to you to beset our society. These might include political and economic issues, social, ecological and technological problems, health and educational concerns – or anything else that you feel strongly about and to which you can suggest some solutions.

4 Write a short fable. In your story you should use appropriate animals to represent various types of people. Your aim is to demonstrate the foolishness of human behaviour, probably by exaggerating it, and perhaps to suggest some solutions.

5 Propaganda. It is said of Squealer that he could turn black into white. Look carefully at how Squealer

organises his arguments and is most persuasive when he
threatens the animals that if they don't believe him Jones
will return – the thing they least want. (See pages 30,
43, and 55–6, for example). Prepare an argument
designed to convince people of the truth of something
they know to be false; for example, that the Earth is flat,
that physical exercise is bad for you or that education is
unnecessary.

6   Collect examples of newspaper and magazine advertising
and show how they use similar techniques to those
adopted by Squealer. These could include the use of
slogans, unjust comparisons with other products, the
careful selection of facts and statistics, playing on the
emotions of the audience and making promises of an
improved lifestyle. Place quotations from the play text
alongside the words and images from the adverts and
summarise what you think is happening in each case.

7   'What if . . . ?' Find a moment in the play at which one
character could have made a decisive difference to the
course of events but did not. Rewrite the scene from
that point, showing what happened as a result of the
character behaving differently. For example, half way
through Act 1 what would have happened if the animals
had started thinking for themselves, as Snowball
demands, and rejected the use of firearms?

C In Performance

1   'Freeze Frame'. This is a drama activity which encourages
you to explore the attitudes and feelings of the characters.
Work in groups of four or five. In your group select a
dramatic moment from the play and cast yourselves as the
characters in it. In turn each group should 'freeze' and
other members of the class must work out which the
scene is and who is who. Discuss what actions and
gestures indicate clearly to the audience each chararacter's

feelings and objectives.

2   Cast the play using well-known TV or film actors. Show why you think a particular actor is suitable by referring to the kind of part he usually plays, his voice and manner.

3   How should this play be performed in order to communicate its message clearly to an audience? In order to answer this question imagine you are staging a production in your own school or college. Devise a set – preferably one that requires no major scene shifting throughout the performance – design the masks for the actors and write the programme.

3 Criticism

1   Orwell is deeply pessimistic about the future of humanity. How far do you agree or disagree with him? Are there aspects of human nature or of recent history and current affairs that would lead you to be more optimistic?

2   All the leading characters in *Animal Farm* are male. Discuss the idea that Old Major's vision and the conduct of the revolution would be very different if women were in control of the farm.

3   An important difference between Peter Hall's play and Orwell's original story is in the ending. Both versions have the pigs and the men indistinguishable from each other and then violently disagreeing, but Hall chooses to develop the ideas of them exploiting genetic engineering at each other's expense whereas Orwell introduces a dispute over cheating in a game of cards. The cartoon version of *Animal Farm* (1955) has a 'happy' ending in which Old Major's vision is fulfilled and Napoleon defeated.

Re-write the ending of the play, from the point where Benjamin reads the single commandment – 'All animals are equal. But some animals are more equal than others'. Write your ending in playscript form. It will need to be dramatically convincing and fit the available characters, but it might also take into account recent events which Orwell was unable to foresee.

4 Look at the events of Chapter 3 in the original story of *Animal Farm*. In what ways has Hall changed the story to make it more appropriate for the stage? What effect does the use of a narrator have on the audience?

5 'Ignore the historical context: *Animal Farm* is essentially an attack on human apathy, insincerity and hypocrisy.' Discuss.

6 '*Animal Farm* demonstrates that it is impossible to defeat a totalitarian government.' In what ways and to what extent is this the message of the play?

7 Orwell is quoted as saying that the most important moment in the book comes when the pigs steal the milk and Squealer is able to justify it to the other animals. Why do you think Orwell felt this was so important? Are there other passages in the play which, for you, are more revealing or significant?

Select Bibliography

All of Orwell's major writing is currently in print and readily available. *Nineteen Eighty-Four* (1949), his final novel, develops the themes of *Animal Farm*. (Both books are published by Heinemann Educational.) His first novel, *Burmese Days* (1935), presents a vivid picture of British colonialism. Orwell is often most powerful in his autobiographical writing: *Down and Out in Paris and London* (1933) and *Homage to Catalonia* (1938) are his two major personal accounts but essays such as *A Hanging, Why I Write* and *Shooting an Elephant* are worth searching out. You will find various collections of Orwell's essays and

journalism in paperback and in the four volume *Collected Essays, Journalism and Letters* edited by Orwell, S and Angus, I.
Bernard Crick's biography, *George Orwell: a life* (1980), is a well-documented, thorough account.

Orwell has attracted a mass of critical writing. *Orwell: A Collection of Critical Essays* edited by Raymond Willams (Prentice-Hall, 1975) is available in paperback, as is volume 8 of *The New Pelican Guide to English Literature* (1983) which includes a ruthless attack on Orwell's reputation: 'The Fatalism of George Orwell' by D. S. Savage.

Further suggestions for teachers of *Animal Farm* will be found in *Focus on Fiction* by Mick Saunders, Chris Hall and Sallyanne Greenwood, and in *Contexts* and *GCSE Contexts*, both by Robin Little, Patrick Redsell and Eric Wilcock, published by Heinemann Educational.

Biographical Notes

Peter Hall was born in 1930 and educated in St. Catharine's College, Cambridge, where he directed many stage productions. He has since directed eighteen of Shakespeare's plays at Stratford and the premieres of plays by Samuel Beckett, Edward Albee, Jean Anouilh, Peter Shaffer, John Mortimer, John Whiting and Harold Pinter. He has also directed operas at Covent Garden, Glyndebourne, the Metropolitan Opera, New York, Geneva and Bayreuth, and seven films, including *Akenfield*. He founded the Royal Shakespeare Company (RSC) in 1960 and ran it until 1968. He has been Director of the National Theatre since 1973, and Artistic Director of Glyndebourne since 1984.

Music
Adrian Mitchell was born in London in 1932. After leaving Oxford he worked as a journalist before collaborating with

Peter Brook on *Marat/Sade* and *US* for the RSC. He has
published several novels and collections of poetry and given
poetry readings in Britain and abroad. His stage adaptations
include *The Government Inspector* (twice), *The Good
Woman, The Mayor of Zalamea* and *Peer Gynt*. His stage
shows have been performed by, among others, the National
Theatre (*Tyger*), 7:84 (*Man Friday*), The Liverpool
Everyman (*Mind Your Head*) and The Nottingham
Playhouse (*White Suit Blues*). He wrote *Uppendown Mooney*
and *King Real* for Welfare State International and
contributed songs to their *Raising the Titanic*. He has
written librettos for three operas and a version of *The Magic
Flute* for Peter Hall at Covent Garden. He was screenwriter
on the films of *Marat/Sade* and *Man Friday*, while his TV
plays include *Cavalcade, Can't laugh, Man Friday, Total
Disaster* and two plays in the BBC's *Churchill's People*.

Richard Peaslee, a native of New York, has written for
the theatre in England and America. He composed the
music for the Peter Brook/RSC productions of *Marat/Sade,
A Midsummer Night's Dream, US, Antony and Cleopatra* and
Oedipus. His music for Martha Clark's *Garden of Earthly
Delights* won him an Obie. Other scores for Broadway and
Off-Broadway productions include *Indians, Boccaccio,
Marigolds, Frankenstein, Cinders* and *The Children's Crusade*.
He has also written music for Joe Papp's Shakespeare-in-
the-Park and theatres such as the Guthrie, Arena, ART and
the Yale Rep. He has composed for William Russo's London
Jazz Orchestra and Joseph Chaikin's Open Theatre as well
as working with Twyla Tharp, the Joffrey Ballet and the
Kathryn Posin Dance Company. He has had concert works
performed by artists ranging from Gerry Mulligan to the
Philadelphia Orchestra. Film and TV credits include *Tell
Me Lies, Where Time is a River* and the Time/Life series
Wild Wild World of Animals.

MUSIC

MAN'S HYMN TO MAN

BEASTS OF ENGLAND

BEASTS OF ENGLAND (continued)

BEASTS OF ENGLAND (continued)

OLD MAJOR

OLD MAJOR (continued)

OLD MAJOR (continued)

ANIMALISM

NO MAN, NO MASTER

NO MAN, NO MASTER (continued)

NO MAN, NO MASTER (continued)

SUGAR CANDY MOUNTAIN

SUGAR CANDY MOUNTAIN (continued)

SUGAR CANDY MOUNTAIN (continued)

SUGAR CANDY MOUNTAIN (continued)

SUGAR CANDY MOUNTAIN (continued)

SUGAR CANDY MOUNTAIN (continued)

ANIMAL FARM

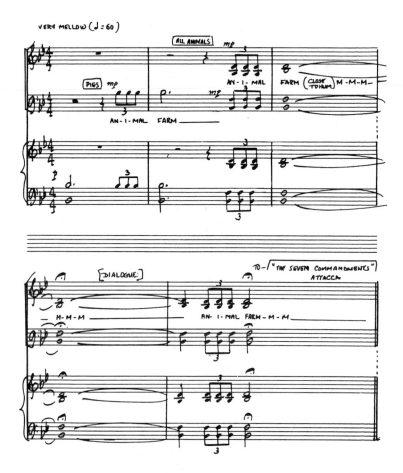

THE SEVEN COMMANDMENTS

THE SEVEN COMMANDMENTS (continued)

THE GREEN FLAG

OUR LAND WAS ONCE A FOR-EST ALL GREEN FROM SHORE TO SHORE TILL HU-MANS TORE THE GREEN-WOOD DOWN WITH AXE AND FIRE AND SAW BUT

THE GREEN FLAG (continued)

THE GREEN FLAG

ANIMAL FARM

THE GREEN FLAG (continued)

FOUR LEGS GOOD

* = ENTRANCES

SNOWBALL ON THE FUTURE

SNOWBALL ON THE FUTURE (continued)

TWENTY-SEVEN RIBBONS (continued)

TWENTY-SEVEN RIBBONS

A VOTE FOR SNOWBALL

LONG LIVE ANIMAL FARM

THE BOULDER SONG

THE BOULDER SONG (continued)

THE BOULDER SONG (continued)

THE BOULDER SONG (continued)

THE BOULDER SONG (continued)

WORK SONG

THE HEN'S REVOLT

THE HEN'S REVOLT (continued)

THE HEN'S REVOLT (continued)

EGGS TO BE SOLD TO MEN THERE'LL BE NO EGGS AT ALL.

LET THE EGGS RAIN DOWN FROM THE HEN-HOUSE SKY

LET THE EGG - SHELLS SMASH LET THE GOOD YOKES

THE HEN'S REVOLT (continued)

THE HEN'S REVOLT (continued)

THE HEN'S REVOLT (continued)

A NOTHING SONG

A NOTHING SONG (continued)

A NOTHING SONG (continued)

A NOTHING SONG (continued)

THE GREEN FLAG: MINIMUS' VERSION

THE GREEN FLAG: MINIMUS' VERSION (continued)

SQUEALER EXPLAINS

COMRADE NAPOLEON

COMRADE NAPOLEON (continued)

RUNT OF THE LITTER

RUNT OF THE LITTER (continued)

RUNT OF THE LITTER (continued)

RUNT OF THE LITTER (continued)

ANYTHING CAN BE DONE

BOXER'S SONG

DETERMINED CHORUS

NAPOLEON RALLIES THE RANKS

NAPOLEON RALLIES THE RANKS (continued)

SOMETHING BURNING

SOMETHING BURNING (continued)

THIS ISN'T WHAT WE WANTED

THIS ISN'T WHAT WE WANTED (continued)

THIS ISN'T WHAT WE WANTED (continued)

THIS ISN'T WHAT WE WANTED (continued)

THIS ISN'T WHAT WE WANTED (continued)

THIS ISN'T WHAT WE WANTED (continued)

TWO LEGS BETTER

I SEE THE FUTURE

I SEE THE FUTURE (continued)

I SEE THE FUTURE (continued)

DIE BUT NEV-ER WALK ON EARTH __ (CHEERING)

I SEE THE FU-TURE SHINE ON ME _____ AND PIC-TURE OF THE TIMES TO

BE ____ WHERE DAY AND NIGHT AND HEAT AND COLD __ AND BIRTH AND DEATH ARE ALL CON-TROLLED __

I SEE THE FUTURE (continued)

Heinemann Educational Publishers
Halley Court, Jordan Hill, Oxford OX2 8EJ
a division of Reed Educational & Professional Publishing Ltd
MELBOURNE   AUCKLAND
FLORENCE   PRAGUE   MADRID   ATHENS
SINGAPORE   TOKYO   SAO PAULO
CHICAGO   PORTSMOUTH (NH)   MEXICO
IBADAN   GABORONE   JOHANNESBURG
KAMPALA   NAIROBI

First published as a Methuen Paperback Original in 1985
by Methuen London Ltd, 11 New Fetter Lane, London EC4P 4EE
Published in the *Heinemann Plays* series 1993
96 97 10 9 8 7 6 5 4

A catalogue record for this book is available from the British Library
on request.
ISBN 0 435 23291 6

Cover design by Keith Pointing
Designed by Jeffrey White Creative Associates
Typeset by Taurus Graphics, Kidlington, Oxon
Printed by Clays Ltd, St Ives plc